Chicago's *HAUNT* Detective

A Cop's Guide to Supernatural Chicago

Raymond Johnson

Schiffer Publishing Ltd®

4880 Lower Valley Road • Atglen, PA • 19310

Designed by Danielle D. Farmer
Cover Design by Bruce Waters
Type set in Viner Hand ITC /New Baskerville BT

ISBN: 978-0-7643-3718-5
Printed in The United States of America

Schiffer Books are available at special discounts for bulk purchases for sales promotions or premiums. Special editions, including personalized covers, corporate imprints, and excerpts can be created in large quantities for special needs. For more information contact the publisher:

Published by Schiffer Publishing Ltd.
4880 Lower Valley Road
Atglen, PA 19310
Phone: (610) 593-1777; Fax: (610) 593-2002
E-mail: Info@schifferbooks.com

For the largest selection of fine reference books on this and related subjects,
please visit our website at **www.schifferbooks.com**
We are always looking for people to write books on new and related subjects. If you have an idea for a book please contact us at the above address.

This book may be purchased from the publisher.
Include $5.00 for shipping. Please try your bookstore first.
You may write for a free catalog.

In Europe, Schiffer books are distributed by
Bushwood Books
6 Marksbury Ave.
Kew Gardens
Surrey TW9 4JF England
Phone: 44 (0) 20 8392-8585; Fax: 44 (0) 20 8392-9876
E-mail: info@bushwoodbooks.co.uk
Website: www.bushwoodbooks.co.uk

Dedication

To the investigator in us all.

Contents

Acknowledgments

Nobody can embark on a journey as consuming as writing a book without the help of countless others. I just wanted to take a minute and thank a few!

The Chicago History Museum research staff

The Newberry Library research staff

The Cook County Clerk of the Circuit Court Archives

The Cook County Clerk's Office

The Cook County Recorder of Deeds Office

The Special Collections Section of the Harold Washington Library Center

The National Archives and Records Administration, Great Lakes Region

Sgt. Eric Shipman and officers of The West Chicago
Police Department

Sgt. Greg Cheaure, Darien Police Department

The Justice Police Department

The Summit Public Library

Chris Breitenbach and Marlene Mark, Morton Grove
Public Library

The Jodwalis family and staff, Willowbrook Ballroom

Chad Griffith and Paranormal Research of Illinois

Mel Doerr (Hi Barbara)

Ursula Bielski

Frank Andrejasich

My mom and dad (Ron and Cheryl Johnson)

My wife and kids (Laurie, Kevin, and Mikey)
(Hey guys! Remember me?!)

Claude and Nancy Daniel (Relax Claude, Nance is in
good hands.)

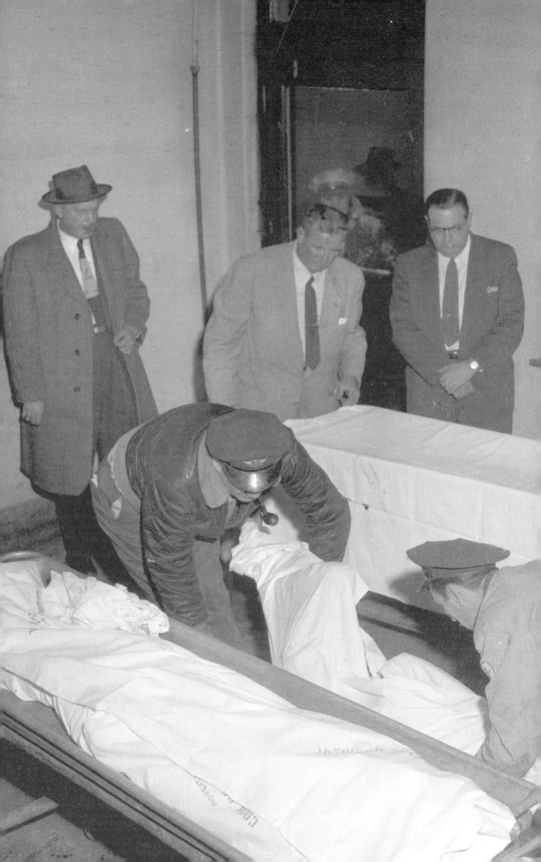

INTRODUCTION

   One of the first things you learn as a criminal investigator, mostly by trial and error, is the importance of having an "open mind." Yeah sure, over time you develop your short list of usual suspects and, truth be told, they account for the bad guy about sixty to seventy percent of the time. That, however, presents a problem. What about the other thirty to forty percent? It becomes clear very quickly that if you stop at the usual suspects, bad things can begin to happen. The bad guy can get away, innocent people can go to prison or, at the very least, have their reputations and personal liberties jeopardized.

When I first thought about writing this book, I knew that having an open mind would be of the utmost importance. I, like everyone else, have prejudices and biases that have built up over time and are sometimes at odds with each other. For example, I have been told that I am a very analytical person, and as an investigator, you are trained to concentrate on the facts of a case: statements, dates, times, witnesses, and other evidence. However, I also enjoy a good ghost story and have had past experiences that I can only classify as "weird and spooky." I once made the mistake of telling some of my buddies at the P.D. about those experiences. A few thought they were cool. A few others thought they should review the results of my pre-hire psych exam.

So what does that mean to you, the reader? What it means is that if you are looking for a book that is attempting to merely debunk some of our most treasured local campfire/sleep-over stories or a book that wholeheartedly embraces the idea of earth-bound "spirits" of the tragically deceased, then you may be disappointed.

I want the reader to be the judge and jury on this one. I promise to present the evidence, as it reveals itself. We will take a journey through some well-known Chicagoland "haunts," take a look at paranormal researchers or the CSI of the afterworld, and see how psychics or "sensitives" have influenced law enforcement over the years. Who knows, we might actually have some fun in the process.

See you on the other side...of the book.

Who is the Author?

Whenever I pick up a book I tend to want to know a little more about the author. It gives me a sense of where they are coming from and any biases or preconceptions that they might have. It also helps me to interpret or read between the lines if you will. For that reason I am including a short background on myself and some of my personal experiences with what I will refer to as the "unexplained." I really hate the terms "paranormal" or "supernatural." Well, I guess "hate" is a rather strong term. Let's just say that I think it gives the reader the impression that it is fantasy or something beyond this realm or natural world. My personal belief is that what we today consider paranormal or supernatural is really nothing more than a very real or natural occurrence that we don't currently have an explanation for. I will touch on that theme throughout the book and don't want to spend much time on it for now, so let's just get on with me.

Me

I was born in the city of Chicago but spent most of my childhood and early adult years in Cicero, Illinois. Cicero is a blue-collar town that butts up to the west side of Chicago. I found it quite interesting as I was growing up, how many people outside of Illinois knew about Cicero. I was pretty naïve about Al Capone until I entered my middle school years and I learned pretty quickly that Cicero was more or less Al's hometown. I guess things were pretty "hot" in Chicago where he conducted most of his business and Cicero was a pretty easy commute.

I was the oldest of three brothers and was one of the lucky ones who grew up in a supportive, happy and I dare say, happy family. My father spent thirty years working for International Harvester and my mother was a nurse. They worked hard to provide us with what we needed and wanted and we grew up grateful. I married my high school sweetheart and spent four years in the United States Army. I was stationed in the "Old Guard" or the 3rd U.S. Infantry at Ft. Meyer, Virginia. Most people know the unit as the Army's Honor Guard and Escort to the President. We had our first boy while I was serving and had our second after I was discharged and working as a manager of information systems for an engineering firm in Westchester, Illinois. I finished my Bachelors degree at the University of Illinois at Chicago and after eight years in the corporate world decided that I really wanted to pursue a career in law enforcement. I had wanted to be a cop since I was in high school but my parents convinced me to pursue my education first and gain some real world experience before attempting that type of career. At the time, I thought they were being overprotective, and maybe they were, but it turned out to be great advice. (Don't let them know; it'll be our little secret.) Starting a law enforcement career with a little more real world experience actually helped to make me appreciate what the police really do and what immense responsibility they carry with them. It also helped me to relate to the public because I *was* the public. I was married, my wife worked, I had two kids and was trying to make a living just like everyone else. I appreciated what it felt like to get a $75 ticket for doing five miles over the limit or "rolling" a stop sign. (Disclaimer:

Chicago's Haunt Detective

You should always obey all state and local traffic laws because you never know when you will come across a rookie with nothing better to do than write a "pimpy" traffic ticket to an otherwise law-abiding *soccer mom.*) But I digress.

I finished my career as a member of the gang / narcotics unit at the West Chicago Police Department in Du Page County, Illinois, and had the opportunity to work with and learn from some of the greatest cops and prosecutors in the state, if not the country. You learn a great deal about the best and the worst of people, and many cops go through life-changing experiences while they are working. Grisly murders, crash victims, domestic violence, child abuse, and sexual assaults can, and do, affect you. You begin to wonder how much of yourself became part of the job and how much of the job became part of you. I personally had the unfortunate experience of having to take the life of a suicidal / homicidal person who had just been released from jail four days before for breaking his girlfriend's jaw. The girlfriend took him back and within four days he was threatening to kill her with a butcher knife. He unfortunately decided it would be better to attack me instead. The shooting was completely justified and probably ended up saving my life and hers, but it is the type of event that many officers go through and there is no way for it not to be life changing. I believe that we really are the sum total of our life experiences and, for better or worse, we are who we are.

I am a Christian and not ashamed of being so. Faith is a big part of my life and my faith has brought me through some harrowing experiences. They are beyond the scope of this book but I mention my faith because when you are dealing with the "unexplained," it is difficult not to bring up religion at times. In fact, an argument by atheists is that the concept of God and a spiritual world is what humans dreamed up in order to explain the unexplainable and that as science progresses there is less need for a "God." I strongly disagree and believe that science and God are not at odds. I look at science as a great tool that allows us to understand a little more every day how great Creation is. This topic is again beyond the scope of this book but I wanted to touch on it because I believe in a "supernatural" when it comes to faith. Consequently, a great majority of the U.S. believes in one religion or another and would therefore believe in a physical world and a spiritual world. Keep in mind that spiritual does not mean "make-believe" or "fantasy;" it merely means beyond what we normally experience in a physical world—in other words, "supernatural." My belief is that much of what we consider to be "paranormal" experiences such as; ghosts, or extra sensory perception can and will be eventually explained by scientific research. It wouldn't make them any less extraordinary or scary. It would just make them explained versus unexplained.

I am also a skeptic. I know that sounds contradictory because most people think of a skeptic as a close-mined, crotchety, gray-haired old fogey who doesn't believe in anything. A skeptic is simply someone who doesn't take as the truth everything that he or she is told or that he or she reads. Cops by nature and by profession are skeptics. They have to be. If you ask Colonel Mustard if he killed Professor Plum in the library with a candlestick and he says, "No," your investigation can't end there! I guess I would have to label myself a "skeptical believer." I say that because I have had experiences that were unexplainable and downright spooky and I couldn't begin a book like this without sharing them with you.

My Experiences
Apparitions

All of the experiences that I have personally had with the unexplained occurred when I was roughly between the ages of 12 and 15. I never wrote down the dates and times or documented them in any written form at the time (which is the problem with most ghost stories) but I have told them over and over again through the years.

Ghost of My Mom? (But She's Not Dead)

I wanted to start with this particular story because to me it was probably what convinced me early on that ghosts and the like may have some reasonable scientific explanation and that they can't all be brushed off as hallucination or dream.

As I recall, it was a summer evening and I was about to start my sophomore

Author's "Haunted" boyhood home—2314 S. Central Avenue. Cicero, IL.

year in high school. My youngest brother and I were watching some television show when I'd decided that I was thirsty. I walked from the living room to the kitchen to grab a cup of my mother's neighborhood-famous iced tea. As I was pouring myself a glass, I noticed my mother in her house coat stirring something in a pot on the kitchen stove. I didn't pay much attention and took my delicious summer refreshment back to the living room to finish enjoying whatever show our six television stations could provide (pre-cable). Since I was of the male species and not prone to multi-tasking, I realized fairly quickly that I had taken the remote with me to the kitchen and to my brother's dismay had forgotten it there. I also made the mistake of not letting him know that I was pouring myself and drink and didn't offer to bring him one back. With a typical younger brother sigh of frustration, he ventured into the kitchen to snag himself a glass and grab the remote while he was there. He came back with his tea but was a little miffed that he couldn't find the remote there. We immediately both went back to kitchen to find it and the first thing that I noticed was that my mother was no longer in the kitchen. I also noticed that there were no dirty dishes from any cooking and the stove was not even warm. At the same time, both my brother and I watched as my mother and father were carrying a large piece of furniture down from the upstairs rooms and past the kitchen. (We had tenants renting rooms from us upstairs.) My mother was completely dressed! I looked at my brother's face and it looked the way I felt. I quickly asked him if he had seen our mother just minutes ago cooking something on the stove and all he could muster was a slight nod yes. I asked my mom if she had just been down in the kitchen in her house coat cooking and she looked at me like I was crazy. She said that she had been helping my dad with the furniture upstairs for the last hour or so. My brother then piped up and said that he had seen the same thing as I had. My mom looked at my dad and said that we were both crazy.

The funny thing is, that you would think that an experience like that would be scary, but neither my brother nor I were actually scared. It was more of an amused confusion. The person or whatever was in our kitchen seemed as real as anyone else. It wasn't a semi-transparent "ghostly" figure that one would assume was a ghost and be frightened of it. The other strange thing was that neither of us attempted to strike up a conversation or attempt to interact with this thing and neither one of us actually saw its face. Was it a ghost of someone else who had lived in the house previously who just looked like our mother? I told this story to a friend of mine who was of the opinion that we may have been peering into a glimpse of the past through a "rip" in time where we were actually seeing something that our mother had done and we were just reliving that time in the present. Whatever it was, I don't believe we ever met this doppelganger again.

Ghost Vandal

The previous account of my mother's doppelganger was not a very frightening experience, but this one is completely different. It occurred in the same house and during roughly the same time period as all of my experiences.

I was in my bedroom, which I shared with my brothers, shortly before I was going to bed. My brothers were not home and I can't for the life of me remember what they were doing that night. My parents were in the living room watching television when I heard a knock on the back door which leads to our kitchen. Once you would exit our kitchen door you would find yourself on a landing which gave you two options. You could walk up a flight of stairs and open another door which would lead to the top floor where we had two boarders renting rooms or you could walk downstairs to the basement or the outside back door.

I was used to hearing a knock on the back door because many times the boarders would be coming down to let my father know about any repairs that needed to be done or to pay their rent. I walked up to the door and opened it only to find nobody standing there. I figured whoever it was changed their minds and I didn't think anything of it. No sooner had I returned to the bedroom (which was the next adjacent room to our kitchen) then I heard the same knock. I returned to the door and again turned the dead bolt and opened the door. Again, there was nobody there. At this point I surmised that one of my friends, or possibly one of my brothers, was playing a practical joke and decided to catch them in the act. (Come to think of it, I could probably consider this my first covert investigation.) I closed the door and did not lock the dead bolt. I even made phony footsteps to make sure whoever was knocking at the door think that I'd again returned to the bedroom. Again I heard the knock on the door. It wasn't a loud knock, just more of polite knock to get your attention. I didn't answer it right away because I wanted them to knock again and be truly committed before

I ripped the door open and caught them red-handed. The second knock came and I tore the door open with a loud "Ah-ha." Nobody was standing there. I could see up the stairs leading to the second floor and the stairs leading to the basement. There was no sound of anyone running or trying to escape my capture. I quickly shut the door, making sure to lock the dead bolt this time and ran back to the bedroom.

I just stood there in the doorway of my bedroom shaking and praying that I didn't hear the knock again. I decided to let my parents know what was going on but before I could leave the doorway of my bedroom the knock continued. I decided that I would not answer it no matter what. There was one series of knocks, a second, and then I think a third and fourth which became increasingly louder. There seemed to be a short break and just when I thought they had stopped, it sounded like someone slammed their entire body into the door in an attempt to knock it off its hinges! This happened in rapid succession, and as I placed my first foot into the kitchen in an attempt to run toward the living room, the back picture window in our kitchen exploded in a shower of broken glass. I met my father and mother running my way almost immediately and they surveyed the damage. On the kitchen floor was a large piece of concrete that had crashed through the window. I tried to tell my parents the story of the knocks and I think they believed me but they didn't really have an explanation either. I believe my father filed a police report for the damage but as you might have already guessed we never did figure out who or what was responsible.

An Explanation?

This ghostly account is very similar to a great many of the poltergeist stories that I have read over the years and some of the theories of poltergeist activity seem to relate that the activity centers around an adolescent child. It is also hypothesized that during this time of hormonal upheaval there may be a chemical trigger that could pre-dispose one to an unconscious ability of telekinesis. In other words, the theory is that a person in the various stages of puberty could be causing things to move with their mind without being consciously aware that they are doing it. It is rather a creepy thought but would explain those situations where people move from a poltergeist-infected house only to experience the same events in the new house. You can't run away from your problems because you have to bring "you" with you.

This next and last account with a "spirit" occurred over the period of a few days. It was in the middle of the night and I was sound asleep in the bedroom that I shared with my two younger brothers. I was the eldest so I had my own separate bed and they, being mere mortals, shared a set of bunk beds. I suddenly woke up very alert. It wasn't as if I was startled awake, but more that I just opened my eyes and I was awake. I looked at the clock which was a large wall clock that I could see on the kitchen wall through our bedroom doorway. My mom did not believe that kids should have a door on their room so she took the door off of our bedroom when we moved into the house and never put it back on. I believe it was because she knew how much mischief could be achieved by three boys behind closed doors. Anyway, the clock hands showed a time of 3:15 am and I was glad that I had roughly another three hours before I had to get up for school and quickly fell back asleep.

The next night I woke up the same way in the middle of the night and out of curiosity I again checked the clock which showed exactly 3:15 again! Even though I admit this was pretty creepy, I again managed to fall asleep and didn't think much more of it until the following night. On the third night I again woke up as wide awake as I had on the previous two nights. This time it was hard for me to look at the clock because I was afraid of what I was going to see. Curiosity again got the best of me and you guessed it, 3:15am on the dot! This time it actually jump started my heart a little and I had a problem falling back asleep.

I know this sounds strange but I had this unbelievable urge to look out my bedroom doorway into the kitchen, so I just stared at the doorway. I tried to look away a couple of times and go back to sleep but it was almost as if my eyes were locked on that bedroom doorway. Suddenly I saw the edge of a large, human-shaped, semi-transparent figure appear from the right side of the doorway and it started passing in front of the doorway as if it were moving toward our kitchen table. It was moving extremely slowly and I stared in shock almost frozen as more of it became visible in the doorway. I snapped out of my frozen state of shock and quickly covered my head with my blanket. (This is, of course, the first line of defense when encountering an earth-bound spirit) I was actually frightened to the point of physically shaking. (Of course, we macho cop types like to call it the adrenaline rush or "fight or flight" reflex. It sounds better than "scared $#&@less.") Suddenly I realized that if this thing wanted to do me harm, my only defense would be a strong offense. I actually stopped shaking and made the decision that I would throw my covers off and run at this thing full force and see what happened. I gave myself the 3..2..1..countdown and away I went. I threw the covers off and without a word ran at this thing which by the way was not fully exposed in the doorway. I remember that I couldn't make out a face or what is was wearing although I know it was human shaped and I could make out only a faint outline of what appeared to be a flannel-type shirt pattern but this thing was colorless. It was almost cloud-like and was hovering off of the floor by about a foot.

I stretched out my arms as if I was an defensive lineman trying to sack a supernatural quarterback and suddenly it seemed as if everything slowed down. It was as if someone had hit the slow-motion button on a video and even the air felt thick. As I got to the point where I actually made physical contact with this thing, it felt as if I grabbed something that was electrically charged. It was very much like when you touched the screen of an old tube-based television set after you turned it off. It was a prickly static feeling. There was also a soft sound that resembled that of a set of wind chimes gently chiming in a soft breeze.

Once I had completely passed through this apparition, everything went back to normal. There was no apparition, no wind chimes, no static, and I was no longer in slow-motion. (Actually my heart was in extreme fast forward.) I immediately ran into my parents room and told them about my encounter which they quickly relegated to an over-active imagination or dream. (I really didn't expect any different reaction and I guess I was just glad that they didn't have me evaluated at the closest mental health facility.

Precognition

It is nearly impossible to talk about ghosts and the supernatural without bringing up the subject of psychics or psychic phenomena. Later in the book I will be touching on the rare instances when police departments and other law enforcement agencies entertain the use of persons purported to be gifted in this area. In specific, I will be concentrating on the ability of persons who claim to have a special gift of being able to receive mental images or feelings from past events through the manipulation of objects or even from long distances away and the ability of persons to "channel" information purportedly from individuals who have died. I have never had or claimed to have had that ability but I have had some psychic events (again during my adolescent years) that could be deemed precognitive in nature. In other words, I've had circumstances where I've "seen" events that had not occurred yet.

Both of the events involved vivid dreams that occurred the night before the events took place. I was not saving hundreds of people from an impending disaster or picking six numbers and a Powerball to win gazillions of dollars (although I'm hoping I will still be able to pull that off one day).

Dreaming in Craypas

In my first dream, I was sitting in my 6th Grade art class waiting for our teacher to start the class. She turned to face the class and announced that we were going to be creating drawings of whatever we wanted using a material called craypas. I had never heard this word before and didn't even know what it meant in the dream but was curious. She handed out small flat yellow boxes that appeared to be the same color as Crayola® crayon boxes. It was a weird cross between chalk and crayon but as I remember was pretty easy to use. In the dream, I was curious about what the other kids in class were drawing and left my seat to walk around the room. I found myself standing behind a girl named Caroline, and for some reason, stayed behind her and watched her create a drawing of the Virgin Mary holding the baby, Jesus. As I said before, the dream was very detailed and I watched her until she completed the drawing. The dream ended and I didn't think about it again.

The next day in art class the teacher announced that we were going to be using craypas and I just about fell out of my chair. Immediately, I remembered the dream I had had the night before and sat stunned for a couple of seconds. Everything about it was exactly as I had dreamed the night before including the seat I was sitting in, the words and actions of the teacher, and even the angle of my viewpoint around the room.

Now I know we are all aware of the concept of Déjà vu, and all of us have had that feeling that we have been somewhere before or have witnessed something before previously, but those are usually very fleeting feelings and only last a second or two. I am also aware that there is at least a scientific theory for the occurrence of Déjà vu which involves our short-term and long-term memories being temporarily "short-circuited," but this was different. I had the entire memory of this occurrence ahead of time.

I decided to test this out and walked over to Caroline's table and stood behind her. I was actually very nervous and almost afraid to look, but to my utter astonishment, I knew exactly what she was going to draw before she drew it. It was almost to the point that I could tell what colors she was going to pick before she pulled them out of the box because I knew what the finished product was going to be before she finished it. It wasn't long before she had finished the exact drawing that I had seen in my dream. I didn't told anyone about that for a long time afterward. I'm not sure why I didn't but I didn't.

Dreaming Goofy

The second occurrence was during the same school year and involved a kid in my class who considered himself the coolest one in the class. He was the typical bully who had his little cronies who flocked around him and used them to torture the less fortunate un-cool kids in class.

In the dream, it is the end of the day and all of the students are in the cloak room. (I don't know if they still use that term in grade schools today, but it was just a little cubby area usually near the door that had a bunch of coat hooks and benches where the kids would hang their jackets and put their snow filled rubber boots.) This particular bully was putting on the goofiest jacket I had ever seen. It was a long, ankle length, white patent leather jacket with a matching waist belt. I really wanted to say something to him about how goofy it looked but didn't feel like getting pounded.

I woke up remembering the dream and how goofy that jacket was and half chuckled to myself.

I probably don't have to even tell you this but I'm going to anyway. The next day in class as we were leaving the classroom and in the cloak room, I just about fell over. This guy was putting on the exact jacket that I had seen in the dream. It was a hideous jacket and I didn't know what was more unbelievable: the fact that I dreamed about this the night before or the fact that he was actually wearing this jacket! Well, I didn't feel like getting pounded in my dream and surely didn't want to get pounded in reality, so I didn't laugh or say what I really wanted to.

I have not had any more precognitive dreams, at least any that I can remember, since my adolescence. I have had a couple of weird coincidences since then such as; when I had guessed the security code of an air traffic control tower when I was in the military stationed temporarily at the Ft. Belvoir, VA Army Air Field (pre 9/11 thank goodness). I was actually eating a box lunch on the air field when I noticed the air traffic control tower security pad about ten feet away. I don't know what came over me. (That curiosity thing again, I guess.)

I just walked up to the key pad without saying anything, punched in a number sequence (I don't remember how many), hit the enter key and presto! The door popped open! I quickly closed the door and the other guys took notice. They asked me how I knew the combination and I told them that I didn't. They asked me to do it again but I couldn't remember the combination. After a couple of failed attempts at doing it again, we decided we shouldn't press our luck with a security alarm.

In another instance I guessed the correct number of coins in a huge jar of pennies that was used at a corporate picnic I attended. Obviously, it could be just a coincidence but I didn't even attempt to count the pennies in the see-through jar and make some sort of "scientific guess." I merely picked up a sheet of paper, scribbled a number on it and dropped it in the box. I had the correct guess down to the penny!

All of these events took place without any conscious effort on my part. In fact, I have never had any luck trying to consciously make any of these things happen. They happened when I wasn't really thinking.

I do not claim to have any special psychic ability, or claim to be able to talk to dead people, or predict the future. I just thought it was important for you as a reader to have a little bit of background about me and my personal experiences so that you understand what I mean when I call myself a "skeptical believer."

What is a Ghost?

That, my friends, is the question that has intrigued mere mortals since, well, we became aware of the fact that we were mortal. We know that primitive peoples took care to bury their dead and showed some form of reverence for their dearly departed, and we obviously still do today. If you doubt that, check out the recent price tag for even a basic no-frills funeral. Death is really big business.

There is also the religious aspect of death and the life after depending upon what religion you profess to believe in. Some of what we believe happens after one dies is based on faith and belief, some is based simply on tradition and some is based on what we see in the movies and on TV. I would venture to say that regardless of what religious or ethnic background one comes from, there is some concern with what happens to us after our life here on Earth has ended. It is really the great equalizer; rich, poor, famous, unknown, young, old, we all have to face the fact that the mortality rate is 100 percent.

The reason I mention this is because I believe that the most commonly held definition of a ghost is that it is the earth-bound spirit, or soul if you will, of a deceased person. The American Heritage dictionary describes a ghost as, "the spirit of a dead person, especially

Double exposure "ghost" photo taken by author's father-in-law, Claude Daniel, in the early 1950s starring his partner in crime, Al Witschy.

one believed to appear in bodily likeness to living persons or to haunt former habitats."

I have been fascinated by the unexplained since I was old enough to read. I am by nature an inquisitive person, which is probably why I gravitated toward a career in law enforcement. I love a good mystery or a good puzzle and let's just say that in my opinion this life after death business is one of the greatest mysteries of all.

In fact, I have found that there are a great many definitions of what a ghost is and I don't think that there is any one that covers it all. There are different terms used to describe a ghost such as: spirit, apparition, poltergeist, presence, soul, demon, angel, and others. We tend to experience ghosts with the same senses in which we experience our physical world. Witnesses have seen, heard, smelled, touched or been touched by what they can only guess is a ghost. I have yet to come across anyone who has tasted a ghost but, to be honest, would probably rather not.

There have been many different attempts at trying to classify ghosts into different categories, but the subject doesn't lend itself easily to classification. There are, however, many different respectable groups that have and still are attempting to study this subject from a scientific perspective. One of those group established in early 1885, The American Society for Psychical Research (ASPR), was established by William James, a philosopher and professor of psychiatry at Harvard University, and other scientists and investigators including, Henry Sidgwick and his wife, Nora, Richard Hodgson, James Hyslop, and Edmund Gurney. The ASPR was born from the British SPR which began three years earlier. These scientists risked their careers and reputation to study the question of life after death. *Ghost Hunters: William James and the Search for Scientific Proof of Life After Death*, is an amazing book written by Pulitzer Prize winning author, Deborah Blum. I would highly recommend anyone interested in the topic to read it. The ASPR still maintains an office in New York and you can reach them on the web at http://www.aspr.com.

Rather than try to classify ghosts, I prefer to see them according to the different theories that attempt to explain them. For instance, the most common explanation of a ghost that I discussed earlier, is that a ghost is the soul or spirit of a deceased person who is, for some reason, still earth-bound and has not "crossed over" into the afterlife. I would call this more of the classic ghost and it assumes that this spirit has a consciousness of its own and can interact with its physical surroundings.

The other major theory is that ghostly or psychic phenomenon can be explained scientifically or with a "perfectly rational explanation." In the case of psychic phenomenon such as precognition or psychic detective work, it can be explained as coincidence, chance, or "retrofitting" where a psychic makes the case match the prediction by using extremely

general predictions which can fit multiple situations. In the case of ghosts or apparitions, they can be explained as psychological deficits or anomalies such as hallucinations, delusions, borderline psychosis, or outright fraud.

I tend to be somewhere in the middle. My personal belief is that there will eventually be a scientific explanation for the paranormal. Not one explanation but various explanations. I believe that there will be a natural explanation for spirits, for poltergeists (noisy mischievous ghosts), for psychic abilities, and the like. That doesn't mean that they will cease to be amazing, curious, or even spooky. Just because we understand genetics better than we did a hundred years ago doesn't make DNA any less wondrous or awe-inspiring. As I mentioned before, I don't believe science and the supernatural or science and religion are at odds. I believe that one helps us to understand and appreciate the other.

CHICAGO GHOSTS

(The Unusual Suspects)

Resurrection Mary

(Chicagoland's Most Beloved Spirit)

It is virtually impossible to pick up a book on Chicago legends or ghosts without running into Resurrection Mary. (No pun intended. Really.) First of all, Resurrection Mary, as she is known, is the Southwest Chicago version of the "Vanishing Hitchhiker" legend.

For those of you who are paranormal newbies, the legend goes something like this:

A young gentleman is out one night celebrating at a local entertainment establishment (tavern, dance hall, ballroom, wedding reception – you fill in the blank). He somehow comes to make the acquaintance of a beautiful young woman. Typically, the young woman is very pleasant but very quiet and mysterious. Toward the end of the evening, the young woman asks for, or the young gentleman offers, her a ride home. At some point before they reach their final destination, the woman asks to be dropped off and can sometimes seem very agitated. The gentleman stops the car, usually in front of a cemetery, and the woman exists the vehicle and disappears from site or simply disappears from the vehicle without getting out.

Sometimes the story goes on further and the woman has either given the gentleman a name or address or leaves something behind that helps identify the woman or the address where she lives. Usually the next day, the gentleman attempts to contact the address where the girl lives to ensure that she made it home safely. At this point, he makes contact with a relative of the woman, usually the mother. He inquires about the woman only to discover that the woman has been deceased for a certain amount of time. Sometimes, the gentleman doesn't even have a name but has the address and while speaking to the occupant, sees a picture of his date on the wall or an end table and is then informed that the photo is that of a deceased relative.

The vanishing hitchhiker, or vanishing traveler before the invention of the automobile, has been around for quite some time. I believe the earliest version of the story can even be traced back to the Christian Bible. In Luke 24:13-32 (forgive me for the paraphrasing) it is said that two Christians were walking on the road to Emmaus (about seven miles from Jerusalem) discussing the recent crucifixion of Jesus Christ when Jesus himself walked up to them and walked along with them. They however did not recognize him. When they got to their destination the two, one named Cleopas, invited Jesus to stay with them because it was almost evening. Jesus agreed and sat down at the table with them to have a meal. Verses 30-31 state: "When he was at the table with them, he took bread, gave thanks, broke it and began to give it to them. Then their eyes were opened and they recognized him, and he disappeared from their sight."

Even though Resurrection Mary seems to fit the general description of the vanishing hitchhiker urban legend, there is something very different about Mary. The people of the Southwest side of Chicago have really embraced her as one of their own and she has gained national if not international acclaim. She is referred to as a "Phantom Hitchhiker" in David Cohen's *The Encyclopedia of Ghosts*, (Dodd, Mead & Company, New York, 1984, p. 293). She is probably one of the best documented and most written about of all of her hitchhiking counterparts. I dare say that she is the most beloved of all Chicago spirits. In fact, just doing some of the research for this book has resulted in my getting threatening emails from individuals who for some reason think that I am trying to defame her or not treat her with the respect that she deserves. (And you thought ghosts were scary...)

So who is Resurrection Mary? Mary receives her name from the Catholic cemetery that is reputed to be her home. Resurrection Cemetery is actually in Justice, Illinois, and its main entrance is off of Chicago's famous Archer Avenue (also known as Illinois Route 171). Archer Avenue has a history that predates the city of Chicago itself. The road used to be a Native American trading route before Chicago was known as Ft. Dearborn and the current road follows the old route very closely. If Chicago can be known as one of the most haunted cities in the world, than Archer Avenue can certainly be known as one of the most haunted roads.

Resurrection Cemetery was consecrated in 1904 and was developed to serve the mainly Polish neighborhoods of the Southwest side. A little known fact about Resurrection Cemetery is that its mausoleum contains the largest stained-glass installation in the world. It really is a phenomenal sight from the inside. Another interesting tidbit is that the Millennium Shrine which was erected in 1969 to honor a thousand years of Polish Christianity was opened and blessed by Karol Cardinal Wojtla who became better known as Pope John Paul II.

The first account that I could find, and the generally accepted first account by Chicago authors and ghost hunters of Resurrection Mary, is the account given by the now-deceased Gerard J. "Jerry" Palus. Actually, local historian, Richard Crowe, who I consider to be one of the first and foremost collectors of Chicago ghost stories and legends, had an opportunity to interview Mr. Palus before he passed away in 1992. Mr. Crowe videotaped the interview and it became part of a 1980s episode of TV's *Unsolved Mysteries* hosted by Robert Stack.

In essence, Palus stated that in 1936 or 1939 depending upon the version you have heard, he was attending a dance at the Liberty Grove Hall and Ballroom in the Chicago Neighborhood of Brighton Park. In the 1930s, dance halls or ballrooms were a very popular form of entertainment in Chicago as they were in many of the larger cities across the nation. Jerry supposedly thought of himself as somewhat of a lady's man and noticed a young, beautiful blond-haired woman in a white dancing dress. He introduced himself and the two spent time together dancing and enjoying each other's company. He seemed to remember that she was very quiet but pleasant and mysteriously cold to the touch. According to the episode of *Unsolved Mysteries*, the girl told Jerry that her name was Mary and that she lived on Damen Avenue in Chicago. As Jerry was driving the young woman home, she asked to be driven down Archer Avenue in the opposite direction of her home on Damen Avenue. While Jerry thought this strange, he honored the request. Mary suddenly asked him to stop the car and let her out. Jerry stopped the car in front of Resurrection Cemetery and the girl simply vanished.

Other versions of the story have Jerry letting her out of the car and she disappears through the gates of Resurrection Cemetery. According to the television program, Jerry went to Mary's address on Damen Avenue and met with an older woman who claimed that a Mary didn't live there. Jerry then notices a photo of the girl he danced with the night before and the woman explains that it was impossible because the photo was that of her daughter who was killed in an automobile accident some time ago.

And so goes the birth of a legend.

Mary Bregovy

Over the years, there have been many attempts to identify who Mary was in life. There have been a few candidates and all seem to fit the bill in one way or another. There have also been a number of different places associated with where Mary likes to frequent. I decided to start with the original dance hall and the original candidate and go on from there.

I would like to make one thing perfectly clear at this point. In fact, this is where I started to receive angry emails from some "over-zealous Mary fans." I am not trying to prove or disprove that any living or once-living person retains the title of "Resurrection Mary." I am simply attempting to compare the different candidates who have been brought forth over the years and how each candidate fits the description or circumstances surrounding the Resurrection Mary of Chicago legend. For all we know, all of the candidates or none of the candidates could be attributed to the legend and at the very least we can agree that it is entertaining to speculate, so please stop sending me electronic hate mail.

With that disclaimer out of the way, the first candidate for that of Resurrection Mary is a young Polish girl named Mary Bregovy, and the first dance hall associated with her was, according to Jerry Palus' account, The Liberty Grove Hall and Ballroom in the Brighton Park neighborhood.

Mary Bregovy was born in Chicago on April 7, 1912, to Stefan and Johanna (Kulawiak) Bregovy. In 1930, the family was living at 4611 S. Damen Avenue in Chicago.

Mary was the older sister of Joseph and Steve Bregovy. Mary worked for Bauer & Black, a surgical supply company, as a factory worker since she was 18 years old. On the night of March 10, 1934, Mary was in a vehicle driven by John Thoel (25) of 5216 Loomis Street, Chicago.

Garage at 4611 S. Damen Avenue where Mary Bregovy's father hung himself.

The Bregovy residence—4611 S. Damen Avenue. Chicago, IL.

Death certificate of Mary Bregovy showing burial at Resurrection Cemetery.

Also in the vehicle were John Rieker (23) of 15 North Knight Street, Park Ridge, and Virginia Rozanski (22) of 4349 South Lincoln Street, Chicago. The vehicle struck an "L" (short for elevated railway) substructure at Lake Street and Wacker Drive. Mary died from severe head injury and shock while en route to Iroquois Hospital (a small emergency hospital started with funds donated from families of the victims of the Iroquois Theatre fire of 1903). Mr. Thoel told police that he did not see the substructure.

For some time, I have read and heard through various sources that Mary Bregovy was buried in an unmarked grave near her mother of the same name at Resurrection Cemetery. In fact I had seen the picture of a grave marker with the name Mary Bregovy with the dates of 1888-1922 in print and on various websites. The claim is that this is the mother of "Resurrection Mary" and that Mary herself is buried either in the same grave or in a nearby unmarked grave.

Using a little genealogical research involving U.S. Census records, Cook County death records, local obituaries, and other newspaper

Grave marker once thought to be that of Resurrection Mary's mother.

Mary Bregovy's father's grave marker.   Mary Bregovy's mother's grave marker.

accounts, it soon became clear that the Mary Bregovy who died in the 1934 accident was not the child of the Mary Bregovy who died in 1922. In fact, she did have a daughter named Mary Bregovy but that daughter eventually became Mary Williams who died in 1987 and is buried a few spaces away. As cited previously, Mary's parents were Stefan (Steven) and Johanna and they did in fact live at 4611 S. Damen Avenue in Chicago.

Mary's parents are buried next to each other at Resurrection. Johanna died in 1945 at the age of 62 of heart problems complicated by pulmonary tuberculosis and Mary's father, Steven, unfortunately committed suicide on September 21, 1951, by hanging himself in the garage of the family home on Damen Avenue. The family was definitely no stranger to tragedy. Mary's death certificate does state that she is buried at Resurrection but a check of the cemetery's computer kiosk will not reveal a burial location. I am sure this is due to the cemetery discouraging the curious or the vandals from dishonoring Mary's gravesite. There is in fact an unmarked gravesite next to Johanna which could be that of her daughter but I did not attempt to confirm that with the cemetery out of respect for the family. This particular Mary seems to fit the age (21 at the time of her death and definitely considered young by dance hall standards). She did die before the earliest recollection (1934), she is buried at Resurrection Cemetery according to her death certificate, and she did die in a motor vehicle accident.

What doesn't seem to match is that it doesn't appear she was returning from or going to a dance at the Liberty Grove Ballroom or the Oh Henry ballroom at the time of her death. (I will discuss the Oh Henry or Willowbrook Ballroom, as it is known today, later in the story.) She died at Lake Street and Wacker Street which is closer to the downtown business district of Chicago. There is also the fact that she had short dark hair and not long blonde hair as almost invariably described in all of the Mary encounters. There also seems to be some disagreement from the various folklorists, historians, and ghost hunters over what Mary should have been wearing at death or during her funeral service. Some like to say that because Mary Bregovy did not die or was buried in a white dress, that it counts against her as being a candidate.

I tend to side with Nora Sedgwick who was one of the original members and researchers of the American Society for Psychical Research. Much of her research was instrumental in the ASPR publication, "Phantasms of the Living." Ms Sedgwick argued that since a ghost or apparition was a representation of the soul or spirit of a person, that a "clothed" ghost was a ridiculous concept. She found it very difficult to argue that clothing or other inanimate objects would find themselves crossing over into an afterlife. I don't think that she was making the determination that the only credible ghost is a naked ghost, but I can see her point that a ghost or spirit wouldn't necessarily be limited to what type of clothing if any that they would be necessarily required to wear. I mean if Resurrection Mary can disappear at will than surely she would be able to wear whatever clothes she wanted to. In fact what self respecting woman would be caught wearing the same dress night after night!

Does Resurrection Cemetery Believe in Resurrection Mary?

As I had mentioned previously, if you attempt to look up Mary Bregovy's burial record at the electronic kiosk at Resurrection Cemetery, you will not find her. There is, however, a way to view cemetery records that many historical researchers know about which allowed me to view Resurrection Cemetery's burial records as they existed in 1989. The records consisted of index cards to burials at the cemetery in alphabetical order. While I cannot include an image of the records in print due to legal restrictions, I can say that Mary Bregovy's burial record was included in the records. Although her name was spelled Mary Bregovi with an "I" rather than a "Y," it was definitely the correct Mary.

Her date of death was listed as March 10, 1934, and the date of burial was March 14, 1934. It also stated that she had died en route to the Iroquois Hospital. I am not going to publish her gravesite information out of respect for Mary and the cemetery's wishes but I will say that she was originally buried in a single grave on the southwest side of the cemetery. She was moved at one point to a new grave location sometime after the death of one or both of her parents. What is interesting about Mary's burial record is that it is out of alphabetical order and immediately before her index card is a handwritten card that simply states, "Resurrection Mary" and below that is written her final resting place!

The Liberty Grove Hall and Ballroom

I was surprised by how little information there was about the Liberty Grove Ballroom. I had read in many accounts that the Ballroom was torn down but used to be located in the Brighton Park neighborhood on the corner of Mozart Avenue and 47th Street. I actually started by visiting the location myself. Today, the corner of Mozart and 47th Street is mostly industrial to the south and residential to the north. The neighborhood seems to be made up of largely a Hispanic population but business names in the area retain much of its largely Polish roots. I initially checked old business directories and amusingly found a Liberty Grove Amusement Company listed at 4615 S. Mozart and managed by an Albert Pavlil in a 1923 Chicago Business Directory. The reason that I found it so amusing was that I found a Liberty Grove Tavern listed at the same address in 1950. It took a second for it to dawn on me that Prohibition was alive and well in 1923. I am sure that calling it a bar or tavern back then would have attracted too much attention from Eliot Ness and his boys.

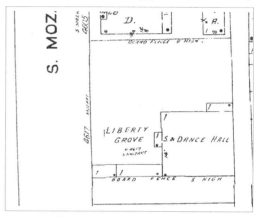

Area of 1940s Sanborn Fire Map showing the location and general layout of the Liberty Grove Hall and Ballroom. *Courtesy of Environmental Data Resources, Inc. and ProQuest Information and Learning.*

There was no mention of the name Liberty Grove between 1923 and 1950 in the city directories.

Today, 4615 S. Mozart is a residential address and I still didn't feel comfortable that I had located the ballroom. All of the accounts put it at the corner of 47th and Mozart. I then consulted a set of Sanborn Fire Insurance Maps from 1919 and saw that almost the entire 4600 block of south Mozart was vacant land. Just south of 47th at the time was a large area called the Gaelic Park and it covered a large area from California Avenue to Sacramento and was set up originally as a sports or exhibition field that had within its fenced walls a dance hall. At this point, I thought that it could be that the Liberty Grove Tavern may have used this dance hall on certain days of the week to hold dances and could have been called the Liberty Grove Dance Hall. It was less than a block from where the Liberty Grove Ballroom was supposed to have been.

It wasn't until I found a 1944 update to the Sanborn Maps that I located what I was looking for. In a 1944 update, I found The Liberty

Grove Dance Hall. It was listed at 4617 S. Mozart and the 4615 address appeared to be that of the parking area. It didn't look like much to speak of. It was a single story, square frame building with a west facing front door and north facing side door. It had a flat composite-style roof. The building was about as wide as a city lot and set back to the alley which was on the east side of the building. The 4615 address represented the parking area and the building and lot were bordered by an eight-foot wooden fence to the north and the south.

It surely wasn't the Aragon Ballroom. The Liberty Grove Hall and Ballroom was more than likely similar to many of what were called Taxi Dance Halls of the era. They weren't much in the way of elegance but it was a way for the young women to make money and a way for certain young men to meet young women. These were the famous 10-cent ticket dance halls. The way it worked was simple. A local tavern owner who could make or clear away a decent-sized dance floor could sell dance tickets to the male patrons at roughly a dime per ticket. The gentlemen would then approach a pool of young women who would dance with them in exchange for the ticket. At the end of the evening the girls would cash in their tickets for roughly half the face value of the ticket or 5 cents using cop math. If a woman attracted enough male dancers they could earn a good amount of pocket money. The concept caught on pretty quickly and soon enough the larger dance halls or ballrooms followed suit and instituted their own version of the "ticket-a-dance" theme. It seemed innocent enough at first glance but I'm sure you could guess at the possible problems that developed. The less reputable establishments soon found themselves in the midst of a prostitution problem and eventually the taxi dance halls and the "ticket-a-dance" program found themselves in the history books.

The Oh Henry Park (Currently the Willowbrook Ballroom)

If you were to poll the newer generation of Resurrection Mary fans and ask them in which ballroom she danced, they would more than likely point you toward the Willowbrook Ballroom on Archer Avenue in Willow Springs, Illinois. There are a number of reasons why someone would point you toward the Willowbrook even though the tale of Resurrection started at the Liberty Grove.

Chicago's Haunt Detective

The first reason involves another candidate for the title of Resurrection Mary, Ona or Anna Marija Norkus. Before we get into Anna's background I would like to finish with the Willowbrook. The second reason is quite possibly geographic in nature. The Willowbrook is geographically closer to Resurrection Cemetery and actually a straight shot south of the cemetery on Archer Avenue by about five to ten minutes, depending on traffic. The third reason and quite possibly the earliest reason for the confusion would be based on the name Liberty Grove itself. If you look back into the recent history of the area surrounding the Willowbrook Ballroom you will find quite a number of references to the name Liberty Grove. In the 1920s and 1930s, there was a Liberty

Oh Henry Park Dance Pavilion, 1923—As Anna Norkus would have seen it. *Courtesy of The Willowbrook Ballroom.*

Grove Pool Room on Archer Ave at 63rd Street owned by the Peters Bros. as well as a Liberty Restaurant at 6244 Archer Avenue which advertised "Tables for Ladies." In addition to that, directly north of the Willowbrook was a picnic grove called the Liberty Grove which was basically at the intersection of Willow Springs Road and Old German Church Road. Today, there is a newer subdivision nestled in the woodlands just north of the Willowbrook Ballroom named "Liberty Grove." There are quite a few references to the name Liberty Grove near the Willowbrook

Ballroom and absolutely none near where the old Liberty Grove Hall and Ballroom was located, so it is easy to see how the confusion could have started.

Oh Henry Park Dance Pavilion interior, 1923. *Courtesy of The Willowbrook Ballroom.*

The Willowbrook Ballroom was established in 1921 by an Austrian immigrant named John Verderbar who came to this country in 1893. John eventually settled in Chicagoland area and loved the relaxed country feel to that area of Willow Springs along Archer

"Out of the Ashes," postcard depicting the newly rebuilt Oh Henry Ballroom after the fire of 1930. *Courtesy of The Willowbrook Ballroom.*

Chicago's Haunt Detective

Avenue. You can still drive along Archer Avenue south of Willow Springs Road and think you are in the country hundreds of miles from Chicago. It really is a very beautiful and peaceful place, even today!

John decided to build his weekend retreat home in this area, and while it was vacant, his son, Rudy, who frequented the dance halls of the era, convinced him to open a dance hall. An idea was born and John decided to rent his five acres of land out for private parties and picnics. The land also included a forty foot by sixty-five foot outdoor dance pavilion! The Williamson Candy Company of Chicago liked the idea and sponsored the venture. The Oh Henry! candy bar is where the dance hall received its name and a legend was born. The official opening of the Oh Henry Park was in the summer of 1921 and it was a big hit. By 1923, the outdoor dance pavilion was completely enclosed and enlarged but in the early morning hours of Thursday, June 26, 1930, someone had deliberately burned the entire establishment to the ground. Amazingly, the Verderbars put together enough money and manpower to rebuild the dance floor before the next Saturday dance was scheduled. It was truly dancing under the stars. By the spring of 1931, the Oh Henry Park had been completely rebuilt at a cost of $100,000 and became the elegant Oh Henry Ballroom.

On January 1, 1959, the Oh Henry Ballroom officially became the Willowbrook Ballroom and had become one of the foremost ballrooms in an era when other ballrooms and dance halls were closing their doors. Even though ownership has changed hands, the elegant traditions of the Willowbrook Ballroom are alive and well today.

I had an opportunity to speak with Birute Jodwalis who, along with her husband, Gedas, have owned the Willowbrook for the past twelve years. I have to admit that when I walked into her office, I was pretty sure that when I mentioned Resurrection Mary that I was going to be escorted out. As luck would have it, I got off easy with a soft smile and a simple roll of the eyes. She and a staffer named Rasa Miliauskas were well versed in the legend of Resurrection Mary. I guess you would have to be if you owned the Willowbrook. Actually, they had a very light-hearted attitude toward Mary and I rather got the feeling that they more or less adopted her when they took over.

Birute was kind enough to allow me to use photos of the Willowbrook from when it was the Oh Henry Park. I wanted the readers to get a sense of what it looked like when Anna Norkus would have danced there. Both Birute and Rasa are Lithuanian like

Anna and know a Norkus family although they don't believe they are related at all. The Jodwalis family purchased the establishment from Richard (Dick) and Patricia (Verderbar) Williams. Patricia is the granddaughter of John Verderbar, the original owner. Birute told me a neat story how on one Halloween night, Dick Williams wanted to test the legend. He had waited until the ballroom was closed and then set a table for Mary in hopes that she might accept his invitation. He waited until 4am but sadly he was stood-up. Oh, those Eastern European girls can be so fickle!

I had told Birute that I was embarrassed to say that I had never been on the inside of the ballroom. It really is something special. This was during the day and it was empty and dark so you really didn't get a full appreciation of what it looks like at night. When you stand on the ballroom floor you get the feeling that you have been transported back in time roughly seventy-five years or so. You can almost hear the big bands playing, and the sounds of people laughing and talking and just enjoying a night out. You can see the couples dressed in their suits and flowing gowns dancing the night away. You sometimes don't realize what amazing places are just minutes from your home and don't really appreciate what you have.

Birute had done some extensive research and discovered that the Willowbrook was the only existing ballroom operating on a regular schedule in the country! Monday and Thursday nights are the only nights that they are not open for dinner and dancing. Even though they have expanded to include salsa and country line dancing, they still have the ballroom and swing dancing that made the Willowbrook famous.

They also still have a full big-band (no recorded music here) and couples that have been dancing there for over fifty years still fill the dance floor.

So how does the Willowbrook become associated with Resurrection Mary? Well, besides the geographic and Liberty Grove name confusion, there is the case of young 12 year old Anna Marija Norkus.

The Willowbrook Ballroom today – 8900 S. Archer Avenue. Willow Springs, IL.

Chicago's Haunt Detective

Chicago Ghosts (The unusual suspects)

Anna Norkus

Anna Norkus was born to Lithuanian parents, August and Anna (Simkus) Norkus in what was then still part of Cicero, Illinois, on September 4, 1914. Ursula Bielski, a local author and historian, has written a number of books on Chicago ghosts and legends and wrote an excellent article on Anna Norkus entitled, "Marija: The half-life of Resurrection Mary." The article appeared on the website, Ghostvillage. com. The, link if it is still active is: http://www.ghostvillage.com/resources/2007/features_03232007.shtml.

Much of the article was based on the research of Frank Andrejasich of Summit, Illinois, who happened to be a distant relative of Anna's.

Anna's induction into Marydom starts on the fateful night of Wednesday, July 20, 1927 (seven years before the death of Mary Bregovy). The story assumes that Anna had recently convinced her father, August, to take her dancing for a 13th birthday present. As retold to Andrejasich, Anna, her father, August, a friend of August's named William Wasnor, and Wasnor's date were on their way home from the Oh Henry when their vehicle struck a deep abandoned railway cut and the car flipped over killing Anna. Even though some details are sketchy, the story as told by Andrejasich is based on fact.

As cited in Bielski's article, *The Desplaines Valley News* did cover pretty closely the Coroner's inquest surrounding Anna's death.

According to the newspaper reports from July 21, 1927 to September 29, 1927, the following occurred:

On the evening of Wednesday, July 20, 1927, August Norkus, 42, of 5421 South Neva Avenue and his two daughters, Anna, 12, and Sophie, 16, were in a vehicle driven by a friend of Mr. Norkus named William Weisner, 32, of 3148 Auburn Avenue. Also in the vehicle was a 14-year-old girl named Loretta Gwozdz of 5312 South Nottingham Avenue.

The articles state that the party was on the way to the town of Clearing which was just east of Summit in order to post bond for an individual who was arrested there. The inquest revealed that Mr. Weisner was driving from the Limits (then the city limits of the city of Chicago) to the town of Clearing by way of Archer Avenue. (In other words they were traveling northeast on Archer Avenue.) They turned right or east on 63rd Street in order to continue on to

Clearing when they met with a *Road Closed* sign at Harlem and 63rd Street. Due to the laying of sewer lines, 63rd Street was closed. There was a wooden trestle with a crude sign written in chalk that directed motorists south to 65th Street.

Mr. Norkus stated that a worker had instructed them to turn south on Harlem Avenue in order to reach 65th Street and they could continue east again toward Clearing. During this time period, Harlem Avenue was nothing more than a dirt prairie road and 65th street was nothing more than a gap in the trees with a ditch. At night, 65th Street would have been nearly invisible. They indeed passed where 65th Street should have been and a few hundred feet later, moving at the blistering speed of 11 mph, the vehicle struck a stay line for a telephone pole and flipped into a twenty-five-foot-deep abandoned railway cut that used to be used

Death certificate of Anna Norkus.

to transport materials by rail to the Argo Corn Products Company. The car landed wheels up and more than likely killed Anna instantly. Anna's father suffered a broken collar bone which was set at Archer Hospital and the others in the vehicle suffered minor injuries.

This particular road hazard was so dangerous that another motorist, Adam Levinski, 58, who wrecked the same day as the Norkus party, died of internal injuries and a broken pelvis the following day after his vehicle flipped into the same ditch. Eventually, it was found that the City of Chicago Streets Department was ultimately responsible for the death of Anna Norkus.

During the course of the newspaper coverage, there was no mention of the party, coming from or going to a dance hall. It was Wednesday night and the Oh Henry Park (as it would have been called then) did have dances on Wednesday, Saturday, and Sunday evenings. Anna was in the vehicle with her father and 16-year-old sister as well as a 32-year-old friend of her father's and another 14-year-old girl who I hope was not his date. It could have been very well that they were coming from the Oh Henry, but there were at least two other dancing establishments in the general vicinity that had Wednesday dances. They were the Toddle Grove, which was a little further south on Archer Avenue (known as highway 4-A), and a place called the Pioneer Relax. It could be just as likely that if they were coming from a dance that it may not have been the Oh Henry at all.

It turns out that Frank Andrejasich was a cousin to a Mary Nagode who was a friend of Anna Norkus. Mary related to Frank that she was pressed into service as a wreath bearer for the funeral which was quite a sad procession. She had made her first communion with Anna at St. Joseph's (Frank's Parish) the year before Anna died. In fact, it was stated that Anna chose the Christian name of Marija as her middle name because of her love and devotion to the Blessed Virgin Mother of Jesus. Anna was buried in a newly purchased family lot at St. Casimir's Catholic Cemetery on 111th Street in Chicago.

The Norkus residence – 5421 S. Neva Ave, Chicago, IL – At the time of Anna's death it was part of Cicero, IL

But how does a young girl buried at St. Casimir become associated with Resurrection Cemetery? It turns out that Mary Nagode's brother-in-law was a man named Al Churas. Al was employed as a grave digger and lived in a bungalow across from the entrance to Resurrection Cemetery. Al stated that grave digging was a very difficult job during those years and labor strikes were common. He in fact had been sent to other cemeteries to pick up bodies that were unable to be buried because of the labor shortage. It was his job to bury the bodies temporarily at Resurrection until the strike ended at which time they could be exhumed and re-interred in their proper burial spots. Unfortunately, the shoddy construction of caskets at the time did not lend itself to easy identification of remains upon exhumation and there could have been a mix up which resulted in Anna remaining in Resurrection even though her marker is at St. Casimir.

Anna Norkus's Funeral Record (Do you Believe in Coincidence?)

Aside from death certificates and cemetery records, many people forget about funeral homes and the private business records that they keep. I thought that if I could dig up Anna's funeral record, it would just be another piece of evidence pointing to Anna's more likely burial location. I gathered from the newspaper reports and death certificate that the mortician who transported Anna's body from the scene of the crash and was responsible for the administration of her funeral was George A. Sobiesk of suburban Argo.

I knew that there was a chance that the Sobiesk Funeral Home no longer existed and it turned out to be a pretty good chance. There were three previous addresses for the Sobiesk Funeral Home and they were all within a one block radius. Mr. Sobiesk had addresses of; 6101 S. Archer Avenue, 6123 S. Archer Avenue, and 7624 61st Place—all listed in Argo/Summit and all no longer funeral home businesses. Many times, if the family does not want to continue in the Funeral Home business, the existing business merges or is bought out by another company.

As luck would have it, I found the Ridge-Sobiesk Funeral Home at 6624 S. Archer Ave. I met with a representative of the establishment and she stated that the funeral home was no longer associated with the Sobiesk family and couldn't tell me if the Sobiesk part of the name was related to George Sobiesk. She stated that the funeral home was corporately owned and that any old records would normally had been disposed of. At this point, I had more or less resigned myself to the fact that I would probably never be able to locate Anna Norkus's funeral record until one fateful night in June of 2010.

I conduct historical research for clients and many times I use Federal Census records as part of that research. When 2010 rolled around, I thought it would be a great opportunity to be part of the U.S. Census process and took a temporary second shift position with the U.S. Census Bureau at the Local Census Office in Lockport, Illinois. After about two months on the job, I happened to be having a conversation with Tom, a co-worker and in many ways like-minded, about really bad horror movies. He said that he and his mother were watching a video last Halloween called "Resurrection Mary" that fell into the category of "Train Wreck." A Train Wreck is when the movie is so bad that you don't really want to watch, but you just can't seem to look away!

I mentioned that I was in the process of writing a book about Chicago legends that included the story of Resurrection Mary and without missing a beat he said, "Hey, my grandfather always claimed that he was the funeral director for Resurrection Mary!"

I couldn't believe what he had just said, so I asked him what his grandfather's name was and he said, "George Sobiesk." I just about fell over. "Do you by any chance have any of the old records from the business?" I asked.

"Sure," he said. "My mom and I were looking at the old ledger books just a little while back."

I asked him if he would be able to bring me the book from 1927 and he said that it wouldn't be a problem. In just a couple of days I was face to face with what I thought I would never see, Anna Norkus's funeral record. In fact, he let me take it home with me which wouldn't really be a big deal except for the fact that I had to drive past Resurrection Cemetery at about 1am with the ledger in my front passenger seat! I don't get spooked very easily, but I have to say that I was just a little uneasy when I was driving past the cemetery with a book that more than likely hadn't been in this area since Anna died over 83 years ago!

Grave marker of Anna Norkus, her father, August and mother, Anna – Anna's photo had been taken off the stone.

RECORD OF FUNE

No... **330**   No... **32**
(Total Number)   (Year Number)

Name of Deceased.. *Anna Norkus* .... **6.**

Wife—Widow / *August Norkus* ....Order Given
Son—Daughter or }

Charge to........

How Secured........ *Cash*

Address..................................

Date of Funeral...........

Residence *5421 So. Neva Ave. Chi, Ill*

Place of Death.. *66th & Harlem*

Funeral Services at..........................

Time of Funeral Service.......................

Clergyman ....

Certifying Physician ....

His Residence ....

Number of Burial Certificate..................

Cause of Death.............................

Date of Death.. *July 20, 1927*
            (Primary)   (Secondary)

Occupation of the Deceased *Student*

Single or Married *Single*. Religion *Catholic*

Date of Birth.. *September 5, 1915*

Aged.... *12*.. Years,.... *10*.... Months,.... *15*...Days.

Name of Father... *August Norkus*

His Birthplace ... *Lithuania*

Name of Mother. *Anna Belankas*
                        (Maiden Name)

Her Birthplace . *Lithuania*

Body to be shipped to........................

Size and Style of Casket or Coffin..............

....

Manufactured by..............................

Interment at *St. Casimir's*

	Price of Casket or
	" Metallic L
	" Outside E
	" Grave Va
	" Burial Ro
	" Burial Sli
	Engraving Plate .
	Embalming Body
	Washing and Dres
	Shaving ....
	Keeping Body on I
	Disinfecting Room
	Use of Catafalque
	" Folding Chair
	" Candelabrum a
	Gloves $..........
	Door Crape $ 2p
	Hearse........
	Carriages to Ceme
	Automobiles to Cer
	Wagon Deliveries
	City Calls (Coache
	Death Notices in..
	Flowers ....
	Outlay for Lot....
	Opening Grave or V
	Lining Grave ....
	Evergreen ....
	Tent or Awning Ch
	Vault Rental ....
	Shipping Charges,

Anna Norkus's 1927 funeral record showing her burial place to be St. Casimir's Cemetery.
Courtesy of the Sobiesk Family.

Chicago's Haunt Detective

Once I got the ledger safely home, I reviewed the funeral record and the place of burial was listed simply as, "St. Casimir."

Could Anna remain at Resurrection even though her marker and family is at St. Casimir? Could it be that Anna is lost and attempting to find her way home so she can be at rest? I can't say either way. I know that I have read about graves being left in locations and not moved such as the thousands of graves that still exist under Lincoln Park in Chicago at the site of the Old City Cemetery that existed before the fire of 1871.

The stretch of road where Anna died is now called, "Old Harlem Avenue."

Bush marking the approximate location of Anna Norkus' fatal car crash at 67th and Harlem Avenue.

So it is very possible that it could have happened that way, however not according to Catholic cemetery records. So, is Anna Resurrection Mary? She died in a vehicle crash possibly on the way home from the Oh Henry Park, however it wasn't the Liberty Grove Hall and Ballroom as Jerry Palus had described.

She was a blond-haired young girl who while not named Mary at birth, chose the name of Mary for her traditional Christian middle name. She was, however, only 12 years old at the time and probably would have been a little young to have danced with Jerry Palus, although I couldn't tell you if ghosts age. If they do, she would have been 22 years old spiritually in 1936, if she was dancing with Jerry at the Liberty Grove Hall. She wasn't buried in Resurrection as Mary Bregovy was, however the possibility exists that she is "accidentally" at Resurrection which is contrary to the information that I received from various Catholic cemeteries. While you mull that over, I would like to touch on a couple other candidates that I came across in my research.

Mary Miskowski

I came across the name of Mary Miskowski in Ursula Bielski's article on GhostVillage as well as a number of other "Mary" websites. The story of Mary Miskowski is told in a couple of different ways. One version states that Mary was a young girl who was killed crossing the street while trick or treating on Halloween night sometime in the 1930s. The other version takes place during the same era but rather than her being killed on Halloween night by a hit and run driver she is poisoned by some tainted Halloween candy. Yet another version of the tainted candy story states that it was her family that poisoned her and blamed it on the Halloween candy.

This particular Mary story was pretty easy to put to rest. There exists no documentation in the State of Illinois records or the Cook County (Chicago) records of a Mary Miskowski of any spelling dying in the State between 1916 and 1950. In fact, there were no Miskowskis at all that died during that time period. I did read one Internet account from an individual who claimed that Mary Miskowski could have been the Mary Muchowski who died on November 5, 1930 according to the Illinois State Death Index. It sounded reasonable since the name was close and a person may not have died immediately after being poisoned or hit by a car, however I discovered that Mary Muchowski is buried at St. Adalbert's in Niles, Illinois, and that she was 67 years old at the time of her death.

I did find one interesting tidbit for what it is worth regarding Mary Miskowski. While I was doing the research on the Liberty Grove Hall and Ballroom, I discovered that the land where it was eventually built was sold in 1923 to the Corporation for the Polish Home of Brighton Park. The Corporation (which never existed according to State of Illinois records) owned the land where the Liberty Grove Hall and Ballroom was built. (Strangely enough, there is also no record of any building permits for any building at 4615 or 4617 S. Mozart until the current private residence was built in 1965.) At the bottom of the document showing the transfer of land was the name of the president and secretary of the corporation. The secretary's name? Mary Myskowska (feminine form of Myskowski).

Mary Petkiewicz

All right, I have to admit that I did not see or hear the name of Mary Petkiewicz mentioned anywhere in the written or verbal accounts of Resurrection Mary. The reason for this is that I had come across this candidate through my own research. I didn't do this to discredit any other "Mary." Again, please do not send me hate mail. I was merely trying to make a point that all of the possible candidates may or may not be the famous ghostly hitchhiker of Archer Avenue. Who is to say that a ghost as well-documented as Mary should only be one ghost. One really needs to keep an open mind. If I learned anything from investigating major crimes, it was that you shouldn't assume anything and you really did need to keep an open mind during an investigation so that you didn't rule out any possibilities early on.

So what about this Mary Petkiewicz? Mary was a young bride and mother, age 17, who was killed in a vehicle crash on Christmas night in 1932. Mary's husband, Casimir Petkiewicz, 21, of 5815 W. 64th Street was driving the vehicle. Casimir's brother, Alex, was in the vehicle as well as Anna Guoinovich, 19, of 5710 64th place; Adeline Ruzzis, 18, and Alcy Neal, 16, both of 6036 South Mason Avenue. Luckily Mary's child, 10-month-old Charles, was not in the vehicle.

It was a dark corner at 55th Street and Cicero Avenue (currently the location of Chicago's Midway Airport). Another vehicle driven by a Mr.

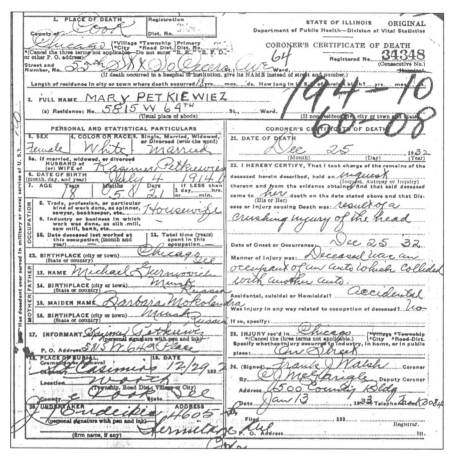

Death certificate of Mary Petkiewicz.

Steve O'Donnell swerved sharply at the intersection and Petkiewicz's vehicle turned over pinning Mary beneath. Steve O'Donnell was the brother of Edward (Spike) O'Donnell, the notorious south side beer boss. All of the victims including some in O'Donnell's car were taken to the South Town Hospital. Mary Petkiewicz succumbed to her injuries and was laid to rest at St. Casimir Cemetery. On November 21, 1933, a wrongful death lawsuit was filed against Edward O'Donnell which was listed as an alias on the court file. Was Edward "Spike" O'Donnell actually driving the car or was Steven's name actually Edward? The answer is not very clear in the paperwork, but what is clear is that the O'Donnells never showed up to court and a jury awarded $10,000 to the estate of Mary Petkiewicz which was never paid. Mary's probate case was closed in 1940 with her family getting nothing from the O'Donnells.

It is probably a good thing that her name is spelled incorrectly either in the cemetery's records or in the state records because I don't necessarily want to create another Resurrection Mary and certainly don't want to send people looking for her grave. (I know it is hard to believe but there are some who are not necessarily respectful of gravesites.)

Grave marker of Mary Petkiewicz.

I believe that Anna Norkus's gravesite was vandalized shortly after her name was added to the list of possible Resurrection Marys. Someone had stolen Anna's photo which was affixed to her gravestone.

My point is that Mary Petkiewicz was killed in a vehicle of other young people on Christmas night. (Perhaps coming back from a party?) She was a very young bride. (White dress sound familiar?) She is not buried next to her husband. (Could she still be looking for him at local dance halls where young people frequent?)

Did Mary Leave Physical Evidence Behind?

I have to again give Richard Crowe the credit for documenting this event so carefully. You can read it first hand in his latest book, *Chicago's Street Guide to the Supernatural*. To summarize the story, on the night of August 10, 1976, a Justice police Sergeant by the name of Pat Homa received a radio call to proceed to Resurrection Cemetery to check on a report of a blonde girl locked inside the cemetery and roaming around. When Homa arrived, he found no sign of a blonde girl, but did notice that there was a section of the bars on the front gate that appeared to have been pried apart, and worse yet, there appeared to be a black handprint burned into the bars!

Mr. Crowe took pictures and had an opportunity to interview Sergeant Homa. I had the chance to see one of the photos at a presentation by Mr. Crowe and I have to say that it looked eerily like a handprint on the bars. I was curious if a police report was ever generated about the incident so I requested a copy of any police report from that day having to do with Resurrection Cemetery through the Freedom of

Chicago's Haunt Detective

Information Act, but was notified that no such report existed. It isn't surprising because generally a report isn't required unless an actual criminal offense or significant incident occurs (especially in 1976). I then had the opportunity to speak with a representative of Resurrection Cemetery and they simply stated that an end loader had accidentally backed into the gate and workers had tried to use a blowtorch in order to heat the bars to bend them back into place. Now my father-in-law was a retired union welder and sheet metal worker so I mentioned the black handprint on the bars and the cemetery story and he said that when a welder is heating up a bar in order to make it more pliable they heat it in sections and it can create an effect called "banding" which he thought could have resembled a black handprint. Whatever the case, the cemetery went through great lengths to obliterate the marks but were unsuccessful until they eventually cut out the section of bars and sent it off to be straightened. I am disappointed that I did not have an opportunity to see this phenomenon myself since I was only 9 years old at the time and probably had not even heard of Resurrection Mary at that point. I will just have to rely on the hard work and resourcefulness of Mr. Crowe.

Chet's Melody Lounge

No discussion about Resurrection Mary would be complete without a mention of a small but friendly establishment that rests just across Archer Avenue from Resurrection Cemetery. Chet's was established in 1965 by Chester and Clara Prusinski and is still run today by their son, Rich and his wife, Barbe. Probably one of the most notorious stories concerning Chet's and Resurrection Mary was the account of a cab driver who had picked up a young blonde fare in a white dress only to have her bolt from the cab and run into Chet's. Of course when the patrons saw the frustrated cab driver and heard his story they knew what had happened, especially since nobody had seen a young blonde girl run into the bar! I had read all of the stories about a Bloody Mary being placed at the end of the bar every weekend as a token of respect and the two "Resurrection Mary" songs on the jukebox but I had to experience this for myself.

I chose to go in on a Wednesday night so that it wouldn't be as busy as a Friday or Saturday night and I might actually have an opportunity to talk to someone. I invited a friend of mine, Bob, to go with me and at the very least we would hang out and have a couple of drafts.

When we arrived there were about four or five other patrons and more than a few seats at the bar. Bob and I sat down at the bar and sure enough at the end of the bar was a Bloody Mary looking very lonely indeed. After a few drinks I asked the bartender, Tony, how long that Bloody Mary had been sitting there and he said that he actually puts a fresh one out every time he works. "Wow," I said. "Has anyone ever stopped in to claim it?" "Na," he said. "The hitchhiker hasn't been around since the 80s."

I thought it was funny that he called her "The Hitchhiker," and in fact he never referred to her as Resurrection Mary the entire evening.

"We don't see the hitchhiker anymore, but there are some pretty weird things going on inside and right outside the bar."

I asked him what he meant and he said that the lights directly above the bar flicker on and off occasionally even though they had the electricity tested, and within the past year, he had encountered something else himself. He actually looked scared as he told me the story. He mentioned to me that he very rarely is ever spooked, but on this particular occasion he was really spooked. He was working behind the bar one night and there was only one young couple in the bar at the time. He went to stand

Main gate of Resurrection Cemetery, 7201 Archer Avenue, Justice, IL.

Chicago's Haunt Detective

outside in order to have a smoke when he heard a young woman whisper in his ear, "Hi, Tony." He spun around because it startled him and there was nobody around. He ran back into the bar and asked the young couple if anyone came in or left the bar and they said that they hadn't heard or seen anyone but they mentioned that right before he ran back into the bar the lights right above the bar flickered on and off!

He then introduced me to a patron by the name of Dennis. Dennis had had his own experience with the bar and coincidentally it also occurred right outside the front door. Dennis had just left the bar in order to have a smoke (I see a pattern developing here) and had been outside about five minutes when someone or something shoved him from behind. He turned around expecting to see a buddy of his but there was nobody there. He was alone and according to everyone in the bar he had been alone the entire time!

Tony said that there are quite a few occurrences of people getting shoved and females having their hair pulled but there has been no explanation that he is aware of.

I did notice that the old jukebox was not there anymore and the digital one that replaced it did not have the Resurrection Mary songs on it. (I was kind of bummed because I thought the music would have really set the mood.) All in all, the beer was good and cold and the conversation was great. It seems to me that whether or not Mary still frequents the bar, the bar seems to have developed a life of its own. But then again, when you are directly across the street from roughly 200,000 departed souls, you would think that a couple of them would stop by for a nightcap.

The fact is you can probably find any number of cemeteries that have any number of Marys who have died tragically at a young age. So I don't necessarily believe it to be extremely important to try to determine who Resurrection Mary is or who she isn't. (Remember, I have had my own strange experiences and have no reason to doubt Jerry Palus or any of the many other witnesses who I have not even mentioned.) The fact remains that Resurrection Mary is one of the most well-documented cases of the Phantom hitchhiker that I have come across and she has been adopted lovingly by the residents of the southwest side of Chicago.

I do know that the next time you find yourself driving down Archer Avenue late one night, if you happen to muster up the courage to pick up a pretty blond hitchhiker, tell Mary I said, "Hi!"

Can You Solve Your Own Murder?
(The Strange Case of Teresita Basa)

It sounds like a great premise for a movie. In fact, I think that it has been used for more than a couple. Well, they say that truth is stranger than fiction, and in Chicago, during the late 70s, it actually happened.

Teresita Basa was born on March 13, 1929, into a relatively affluent family in the Phillipines. She had immigrated to the United States and was employed at Edgewater Hospital on the north side of Chicago as a respiratory therapist. She had never been married and was living alone on the 15th Floor of an apartment building on North Pine Grove Avenue. She had a great love for music and was in the process of writing a book in hopes of being hired into a faculty position teaching music at the University level.

All that changed when the screaming of fire engines pierced through the neighborhood on the night of February 21, 1977. The fire crews raced up to Apartment 15B at 2740 N. Pine Grove Avenue to find the nude, partially burned body of Teresita with a large kitchen knife protruding from her chest.

Detectives Joseph Stachula and Detective Lee Epplen from Area 6 Homicide were assigned to the case. Several leads were followed and after a couple of months, the case pretty much went cold. That was until Detective Stachula found a note on his desk from the Evanston Police Department to contact a Dr. Jose Chua in Skokie, Illinois regarding the Teresita Basa case. What Detective Stachula would discover soon became a major story covered by national newspapers. In fact, John O'Brien and Edward Baumann of the Chicago Tribune covered the story and eventually in 1992 wrote a book entitled, *Teresita – The Voice From the Grave* (Bonus Books, Inc., Chicago). Those newspaper articles, the book, a review of the court

Teresita Basa's apartment at 2740 N. Pine Grove Avenue, #15B – 15th floor balcony on the left.

case, and visiting the locations of the story is how I conducted most of the research for this account.

Dr. Chua had related to Detective Stachula that a number of months after the killing of Teresita, his wife, Remedios "Remy," had started having visions of Teresita and was seemingly "possessed" by the spirit of Teresita Basa. Dr. Chua recounted how, on a number of occasions his wife had fallen into an almost comatose trance and the voice of Teresita had come from his wife's mouth. He stated that the

Showery's residence at the time of the murder, 445 W. Surf Street, Chicago, IL.

voice was actually speaking Spanish and he and his wife did not speak Spanish. They spoke Ilocano and Tagalog, the national language of the Phillipines. He revealed that at first the voice simply stated that its name was Teresita and it needed Dr. Chua's help to solve the murder case. It wasn't until Dr. Chua demanded proof that the voice, during subsequent "possessions," had named her killer as Allan Showery. The voice stated that Allan had come to Teresita's apartment that night to fix her television set and that he had killed her. The voice also stated that Showery had taken jewelry from her apartment and had given that jewelry to his girlfriend. The voice specifically mentioned that the jewelry was purchased in France and that it was a gift from Teresita's

father to her mother. As if that wasn't extraordinary enough, the voice also supplied the names of Ron Somera, Ken Basa, Richard Pessotti, and Ray Kings as individuals who could identify the jewelry as Teresita's. It not only supplied the names of the individuals but their phone numbers as well!

I can definitely empathize with what must have been going through Detective Stachula's mind at this point. In one sense, it was a fresh lead in an unsolved murder case; but on the other hand, he had to face the onslaught of almost guaranteed unending ribbing by not only his partner but the other detectives at Area 6. Believe me, I know from experience that there is no group of individuals better trained to mess with your head than the same group of individuals that would take a bullet for you if need be. Police officers have honed the craft of "cranking you" into a veritable form of art and roam the hallways of the station like a pride of lions looking for a sick or injured wildebeest. I have been that wildebeest and I know that Stachula was feeling the antlers sprouting from his head at that very moment.

As it turned out, Remy Chua was also a respiratory therapist at Edgewater Hospital and knew Teresita. They had worked different shifts, but she considered her an acquaintance though not a particularly close one. She had been to Teresita's apartment once before when Teresita had thrown a party after she passed her respiratory therapist tests but didn't socialize much with her on a regular basis at all. Remy also knew of Allan Showery who was a thin muscular orderly who claimed to be a martial arts expert and Vietnam veteran and made her feel uncomfortable at times.

Edgewater Hospital, where Basa, Chua, and Showery all worked together, 5700 North Ashland Avenue, Chicago, IL.

Stachula returned to his desk and after finishing his report on the interview with the Chuas asked to have a records check done on Allan Showery. After a short time, it was discovered that Showery had a history of arrests from New York on rape charges. Showery and Epplen decided they had enough information to at least talk to Showery.

On August 11, almost six months after the murder, they arrived at 630 W. Schubert. At the time of the murder, Allan had lived at 445 W. Surf Street which was roughly four blocks from Teresita's apartment building. Currently Showery was living on the second floor of the Schubert address with his common-law wife, Yanka Kamluk. The detectives met with Kamluk and Showery

Showery's second floor residence at the time of his arrest, 630 W. Schubert Avenue, Chicago, IL.

inside the apartment. They informed him that they were investigating the death of Teresita Basa and they asked him if he could come to the police station to help them shed some light on some of the questions that they had. Showery accompanied them voluntarily while Kamluk remained in the apartment. Once at the police station, Stachula and Epplen, who had worked together for quite a while, went into interview/interrogation mode. They managed to snare Showery into a number of his own lies. At first he had denied ever being in Basa's apartment but later recanted when he realized that fingerprints could put him at the scene. They were amazed at how much Remy Chua, or Teresita, depending on what you believe, was right on the money! They had a statement by Showery that he had returned home the night of the murder to work on an electrical problem after Basa had supposedly told him by telephone that she couldn't meet with him that night to fix her television set.

They decided to put Showery on ice and return to the apartment to question Kamluk.

At the apartment Kamluk stated that she remembers the night of the murder because of the fire engine sirens. She denied that Showery had done electrical work that night and didn't even believe that he knew anything about electricity. They also asked her if Showery had recently given her any gifts and she stated that he had given her a ring as "a late Christmas present" as well as a jade pendant. The detectives observed the jewelry in question and immediately made the phone calls to the family members of Basa that Remy had identified during one of her "possessions." They asked Kamluk if she would come down to the station to help calm Showery's nerves and she agreed. Kamluk was wearing the ring in question and when Teresita's relatives arrived they positively identified the ring as hers.

Faced with the evidence confronting him, Showery caved and gave a full confession.

Showery arrived at Teresita's apartment as planned around 7:30pm the night of February 21, 1977. This fact was confirmed by a telephone call that Teresita's friend, Ruth Loeb, made to Teresita that night around 7:30pm. Teresita indicated in the phone call that she was entertaining a male friend but didn't say who. He waited for her to lock the door and then grabbed her from behind and placed her in a "Japanese Half-Nelson" choke hold. Showery was a student of the martial arts and was in relatively good shape. According to Showery, she passed out and he placed her on the bed. He stripped off her clothes in an attempt to make it appear as if it was a rape/murder. He denied sexually assaulting her and that fact was confirmed by the autopsy which showed that Teresita was a virgin. He then went to the kitchen to retrieve a kitchen knife, straddled over her body and thrust the knife deep into her sternum. He then ransacked the house and was only able to make off with $30 and a couple of items of jewelry which he later gave to Kamluk. He then lit a paper bag on fire, ignited the mattress and turned it over on her body. He immediately left the apartment and stated that no one had seen him leave.

Allan Showery was officially charged and held for seventeen months at the Cook County Jail in lieu of a $500,000 bond. The trial itself started on January 21, 1979, and made national news. Four weeks later the jury found itself hopelessly deadlocked and a mistrial was declared. The Chuas were concerned about the possibility of Showery being released and exacting some type of revenge but Showery surprised everyone including his attorneys by pleading guilty to the murder on February 23, 1979, almost two years to the date of Teresita's death.

Showery was sentenced to fourteen years for the murder and four years each for two counts of aggravated arson and robbery but was paroled in July 1983 after serving only four and one half years.

Did the restless spirit of Teresita Basa, angered at the fact that her murderer would go unpunished, possess the person of Remy Chua? Did Remy possess some sort of psychic connection to the events of the murders? Showery didn't think so. John O'Brien had the opportunity to interview Showery before he was sent to the penitentiary and Showery believed that Remy Chua had an axe to grind. He stated to O'Brien that he had complained about Remy's work at the hospital and it eventually led to her being fired. He also stated that Remy was aware that he had been reading magazines on the supernatural and occult and in his opinion made up the whole story.

I'll have to admit that on the surface the case sounds remarkable but when I try to look at it as a "skeptical believer" I feel differently. Shortly after the case concluded, the Chuas agreed to have a friend of theirs, foot surgeon Dr. O.A. Mercado and his wife Carol, write their story. The book entitled, *A Voice from the Grave* was published in 1979. (The Berkley Publishing Group, New York)

In the book, Remy relates to a couple of instances where Showery had frightened her with comments about the martial arts or being a Vietnam veteran. She, and according to the book, a number of other workers at the hospital, thought Showery to be a creepy individual. Remy relates one instance where she snaps at Showery and he asks her why she hates him so much.

In my opinion, Remy had too much personal familiarity with Teresita and Showery as well for the whole situation to be attributed to psychic knowledge. I am not saying that the Chuas were lying or wanted all of the ensuing publicity that resulted from the case. I am merely saying that most, if not all, of the claims could be explained in more non-pychic terms.

Remy admits that she knew Teresita and in the Mercado's book mentions a time when Teresita asked her how it felt to make love to a man. In police work we would call that a clue! If someone were to ask me that question, I would have to assume that the girl was a virgin. The fact that Remy was a virgin came up as a result of the autopsy and was one of the factors that supposedly led to the "possessions" being authentic because there was no mention of a sexual assault in any of the questionings of "Teresita."

Remy also admitted being at a party thrown by Teresita following the passing of her respiratory therapist exams. She knew what the inside of Teresita's apartment looked like. She worked with Teresita and had conversations with her of a personal nature. She had ample opportunity to see Teresita's jewelry and possibly the story behind the jewelry. She worked along with the murderer, Allan Showery. She was frightened by him and had confrontations with him prior to her "possessions."

In my opinion, and again this is only my opinion, it is more likely that Remy had suspicions that Showery had something to do with Teresita's death. She possibly overheard the fact that he was going there that night to fix the television and was afraid that Showery may figure out that she knew too much and would kill her as well. It is possible that maybe she was aware of Showery's girlfriend having Teresita's jewelry and was also worried that Showery possibly knew. It could be that Remy was trying to protect her family from retribution by claiming that the information came psychically thereby saving her family from the revenge of Showery and at the same time clearing her conscience by pointing the police to the murderer and just letting them do their job. Remy may have accomplished all of this without even consciously realizing that she was behind the possessions herself, or I should say her subconscious might have been behind the possessions. I think the case for a psychic link or possession would have been stronger had Remy Chua not had any knowledge or history with either Teresita Basa or Allan Showery.

Whatever your beliefs are, the end result was the same. Allan Showery was brought to justice for the crime he committed although I don't believe the punishment (only roughly fifty-four months behind bars) fit the heinous crime that it was. We must however take solace in the fact that we will all meet the ultimate judge one day and that justice, unlike our own, is perfect.

Chicago's Haunt Detective

Innocence Lost
(The Grimes Murders and the Ghosts of German Church Road)

Chicago is no stranger to murder. In fact, the last word that most people would use to describe Chicago is innocent. One does get the feeling however that after the murder of the teenage Grimes sisters, the general carefree feeling of family life in Chicago during the 1950s came to a screeching halt. This particular case still brings shudders and strong emotions to those who remember it.

Fifteen year old Barbara Jeanne Grimes and her thirteen year old sister, Patricia Kathlene Grimes were two of the six children of Joseph and Loretta Grimes of 3634 S. Damen Avenue in the

The Grimes family residence, 3634 S. Damen Avenue, Chicago, IL.

Brighton Park neighborhood of Chicago. Joseph Grimes was a union truck driver and Loretta worked as a clerk for the Parke Davis & Co., pharmaceutical company on Franklin. At the time of the murders, Joseph and Loretta had been divorced for eleven years and Joseph was remarried. Patricia and Barbara had a married older sister named Shirley Wojcik, 30, an older sister Theresa, 17, and two brothers, Joseph, 14, and James, 11.

By all accounts, Barbara and Patricia were average run-of-the-mill teenage girls. Barbara was a sophomore at Kelly High School and Patricia was a seventh grader at St. Maurice School.

At about 7:30pm on the night of December 28, 1956, the girls left their home with $2.50 between them. Their plan was to see the newly released Elvis Presley movie for the 15th time. When the girls failed to return home on time, their mother left the house to look for them. A girl friend by the name of Carol had told Mrs. Grimes that she last saw the girls in the Brighton Park Theatre, 4223 Archer Avenue, at 10:30pm. Carol said that the girls were not planning on leaving the theatre yet because they had not seen the complete movie. Another friend by the name of Dorothy Fisher had confirmed seeing the girls in the theatre at around 10:30pm as well. She didn't know it yet, but Mrs. Grimes would never again see her girls alive.

Pictures of the girls appeared in the newspapers the following day with their descriptions. Barbara, the older but shorter girl was 5 feet tall with brown hair and eyes. She was wearing black ballerina shoes, size 5½, gray tweed skirt, waist size 22 or 24, with a label bearing the name Robinson, State and Jackson, Chicago, a yellow blouse, ¾-length gray car coat size 12 or 14, with a Robert Hall label, white bobby sox, and a gray babushka. Patricia was 5-foot-3 inches tall also with brown hair and eyes. She was wearing black shoes size 8 ½ or 9, blue jeans, a black jacket with a white stripe on the sleeves and a white babushka.

What was to follow was one of the most labor intensive missing persons case in Chicago history. The sisters went missing on Friday night and by Sunday there were no less than fifty policemen combing the South-west side neighborhood. Eventually, the operation would use hundreds of police officers, thousands of man hours and flyers, task forces including officers from neighboring towns such as La Grange,

Patricia and Barbara Grimes had gone to see the Elvis Presley movie, Love Me Tender, at the Brighton Theater, 4223 Archer Avenue, Chicago, IL. *Courtesy of The Chicago History Museum of The Chicago Historical Society.*

The Brighton Theatre is only an empty lot today.

Chicago's Haunt Detective

Justice, Bridgeview, Summit, Bedford Park, Willow Springs, and The Forest Preserve police. Thousands of circulars were distributed with the girls' photos, and Elvis Presley himself appealed to the sisters over the radio.

The police initially surmised that the girls had probably run away. Loretta was never of that opinion. She said that the girls had no reason to run away and it wouldn't make any sense that they would leave all of their possessions behind including many Christmas presents that included treasured portable radios as well as all of their clothing.

Reports of persons seeing the girls came pouring into the police department. There were reports of persons seeing the girls as far away as Nashville, Tennessee. At one point a person by the name of Jack Franklin, 68, of 3647 Ainslie Street, supposedly saw the girls on Lawrence Avenue near Central Park Avenue. This was roughly the same location that 3 boys who similarly disappeared back on October 16, 1955 were last seen alive. The boys, Robert Peterson, 13, and brothers John, 13, and Anton, 11, Schuessler were found dead two days later in the Robinson Woods Forest Preserve. With this new information, Chief of Detectives Patrick Deeley's triple killing unit was assigned to the case as well as forty men from each shift at the Brighton Park police station, twelve men from the juvenile bureau, and detectives from the sex, homicide, and burglary details.

The family, including an older married sister, Shirley Wojcik, 27, and older sister Theresa, 17, maintained that they came from a happy home and had no reason to leave voluntarily. Sister Ritella, O.S.F. who was the principal at St. Maurice School said that the girls always had "fair marks" and that they were no trouble in school. Friends described the girls as friendly and outgoing and nobody recalled them being upset or troubled to the point that they would become runaways.

As reports and sightings continued to come in, the police tried to put together a timeline of the sightings. The following partial timeline was compiled using reports from *The Chicago Tribune* as well as *The Chicago Daily News:*

> *On December 28, 1956, the girls departed their home at 7:30pm to see a movie at the Brighton Theatre, 4223 Archer Avenue.*

> *At 10:30pm both sisters were seen by a friend, Dorothy Fisher, 15, in the theatre sitting together.*

At 11:05pm, a CTA bus driver believed he saw the sisters get off his Archer Avenue bus at Western Avenue.

Kelly High School attended by Barbara Grimes.

On December 29, 1956, at 9:40am, Jack Franklin, 68, reported two girls resembling the sisters at a bus stop at Lawrence Avenue and Central Park Avenue.

At 6:30pm, Catherine Borak, 13, a classmate of Patricia, reported that she saw Patricia walk past a restaurant that she was in at 3551 Archer Avenue in the company of two other girls that she didn't recognize.

St. Maurice School attended by Patricia Grimes.

On January 1, 1957, at 2:30pm, Robert Curran, a CTA bus driver, told police that the sisters were on his bus on Damen Avenue. Also on January 1st, a North Shore motorman, Bernard Norton, said two girls who looked like the Grimes girls boarded his train at the Edison Court Station in Waukegan at 2:00pm on Sunday. The station was two stops north of the Great Lakes Naval Training Center.

Police began investigating the possibility that the girls could be with a couple of sailors that they had met at the Oriental Theatre. Mrs. Grimes remembered that their names were Terry and Larry and that the girls had brought them to the house for coffee and cake. She mentioned that the last time they called the girls was on November 28th.

On January 2, 1957, at 9pm, George Pope, a clerk at the Unity Hotel, 750 W. 61st place, said the sisters asked for a room but were refused.

On January 3, 1957, at 2:00pm, three employees in a S.S. Kresge (predecessor of K-mart) store, 6300 S. Halsted Street, reported sisters hanging around the record counter and playing Elvis Presley records.

On January 5, 1957, police received reports from a number of Chicago areas and suburbs that the sisters had been seen.

Chicago's Haunt Detective

Chicago Ghosts (The unusual suspects)

On January 8, 1957, Illinois State Police reported that a junk dealer in Gilman, Iroquois County, said he saw two girls about 14 and 15 in Gilman with two men in a dirty maroon 1947 model car with Tennessee license plates and a Chicago sticker. The Brighton Park police stated that they were almost convinced that the two sisters visited Memphis, Tennessee, the hometown of their idol Elvis Presley, after a number of Memphis citizens identified photos of the sisters as having asked for jobs or been at bus depots.

On January 10, 1957, an anonymous call was received by Henrietta Marshall, a switchboard operator at the Catholic Youth Organization, 1122 S. Wabash Avenue. The caller stuttered and then asked if she knew the parking lot in Grant Park near the Grand Central Station. He then asked for a priest. The caller stated, "Tell the priest I'm sorry, that I couldn't help it. But there is a 13 year old girl tied up in the trunk of my car in the parking lot." The Chicago police sent squads to the Central Station at Roosevelt Road, the Field Museum area, the Grand Central station parking lots, the Monroe Street lot and the Grant Park underground garage. All in all over 3,000 cars were searched but no girl was found in any trunk.

On January 15, 1957, an anonymous phone call was made to the Chicago Police Department's main complaint line at 1121 S. State Street from a tavern at 6108 S. Halsted Street. Detectives William O'Malley and Frank Hackel learned that a man by the name of Walter Kranz, 53, of 5949 Halsted Street and a man by the name of Stanley Cerwicz, 38, of 5422 Aberdeen Street had used the phone and were patrons of the tavern at the time the call was placed. The caller stated that police could find the bodies of the Grimes girls in Santa Fe Park. Santa Fe Park was in the village of Tiedtville and was where stock car races and motorcycle races took place. An article in the Chicago Tribune, dated January 23, 1957, states that police described the Santa Fe Park as, "an area frequented by youths and men sporting long sideburns, and flat top and duck tail haircuts." (Scary huh?) Detectives O'Malley and Hackel brought Kranz in for questioning. He told them that he was a steam fitter who had been divorced for three years. He also told them that he was a Marine Corps. Veteran of World War II, a moderate drinker, and was paying his ex-wife and three children alimony of $45 per week. Kranz was released after questioning during which he denied making the phone call to police.

In the early afternoon of January 22, 1957, Leonard Prescott was driving east on German Church Road on his way to the grocery store when he noticed what he thought were a couple of mannequins lying at the side of the road a short distance east of County Line Road. He didn't stop but went back home to get his wife, Marie. The two returned to the scene and confirmed that the two mannequins were actually the nude bodies of two young girls. They drove to the Willow Springs police department and reported what they found at approximately 1:30pm.

The Grimes sisters' bodies were discovered just on the other side of the guardrail along this stretch of Old German Church Road.

What happened next was somewhat of a media circus. Investigators, press, and curiosity seekers converged on the scene jeopardizing the integrity of the crime scene. (Today the scene would have been secured and cordoned off so as not to destroy any possible evidence.) Three of the first investigators on the scene were Harry Glos, chief investigator for the coroner's office (now called the medical examiner's office), Sheriff Joseph Lohman and Undersheriff Thomas Brennan.

One girl was lying in a north-south direction on her left side while the other girl was lying on top of her at a right angle. The girls' father identified the body on top as that of Barbara although Glos stated it was Patricia. Glos stated that the body of Patricia had three puncture

An exhausted Loretta Grimes looks at her girls' pictures on the recently distributed 'missing' flyer. Author's personal collection.

wounds in the chest area that resembled those that would be made by an object similar to an ice pick. Barbara, on the bottom had looked as though she had bruises on her cheek and possibly a broken nose.

The autopsy would have to be delayed to give the bodies a chance to adequately thaw due to the harsh January temperatures of Chicago. The investigators formed the opinion that the girls had more than likely been in that position since the heavy snows of January 9th and 10th and the recent thaw had revealed the horrific sight.

In the meantime, the hunt was on for the killer or killers. There were 200 law enforcement officers that combed the area near where the girls were found and also the area of Santa Fe Park. Walter Kranz was re-arrested by Chicago police and brought in for more questioning. He was given two polygraph tests by technician Walter Gehr. During the first test Kranz denied making the phone call once again but the test indicated deception. In fact, Gehr stated that Kranz gave unsatisfactory answers to most of the key questions concerning the killings. On the second test, Kranz admitted making the anonymous phone call to the police claiming that the girls could be found in Santa Fe Park. Kranz stated that he made this claim because of a dream that he had of seeing the girls' bodies there. Kranz was held pending the results of a third test scheduled for the evening of January 23rd.

The other patron of the tavern the night Kranz made the phone call, Stanley Cerwicz, was picked up at his home and brought in for questioning. He was given a polygraph test and police determined that he knew nothing of the killings, was not associated with Kranz, and was released.

At about the same time, another suspect was identified. Twenty-one-year-old Edward Lee (Bennie) Bedwell was described by his mother, Ethel Bedwell Bradbury, as being a lazy, shiftless bum. His father, John Bedwell of Paris, Tennessee, and Ethel had divorced in 1937, and Ethel was currently married to Curtis Bradbury, a sewer repairman living at 1430 Monroe Street. Edward (Bennie) had come to Chicago after a brief eight to ten month stint in the Air Force which ended with him claiming an injury to his knee after falling in the Barracks. Bedwell worked as a part-time dishwasher at the D&L Restaurant at 1340 Madison Street. Mr. John Duros and his wife Minnie owned the restaurant and reported that they had seen Bedwell with the Grimes girls and another unidentified man of "swarthy" or dark complexion at two separate times on the morning of January 6th.

This fact was also confirmed by a cab driver, Reno Voldis Echols, 27, of 1355 Madison Street who stated that he remembered seeing the

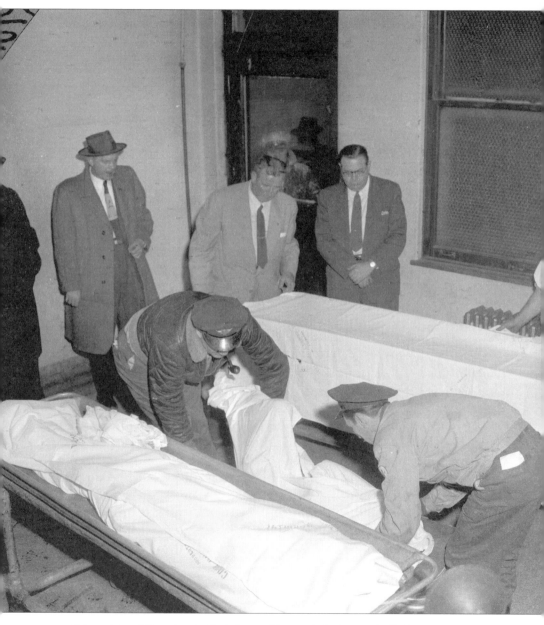

Grimes sisters delivered to the Cook County Morgue. *Author's personal collection.*

girls in the company of two men between 4am and 5am on that Sunday, January 6th in a back booth of the restaurant. He remembers that the girls left with one of the men. Both Mrs. Duros and Echols identified pictures of the Grimes sisters, and Mr. Duros said that he recognized them from their pictures in the newspapers.

Mrs. Duros stated that Bedwell arrived at the restaurant at about 5:30am with the two girls and the other man. She said that the girl she recognized as Barbara appeared "sick or doped" and the other she believed to be Patricia appeared as if she had been drinking. After the group left, Barbara ran back in upset and said that she was being forced into a car. She sat in a booth with her head in her hands when Patricia came back in to "rouse" Barbara. Mrs. Duros stated that she told Patricia to leave her alone and Patricia answered, "This is my sister." After that, the two men returned and carried Barbara out by supporting her under her arms.

According to Mr. Duros, the two men returned with the girls at about 9:30am. He said that Bedwell and Barbara were carrying on and he asked them to leave. Bedwell paid the bill and they left.

Bedwell came back to the restaurant a couple of days later alone. Mr. Duros asked him what he did with the girls and Bedwell answered, "We got 'em." He told Bedwell that he better turn the girls over to the police or it would be his neck. Bedwell hung his head and left the restaurant.

Bedwell's full-time job was as a machine operator at the Ajax Consolidated Company at 4615 W. 20th Street. Company records indicated that he had worked until 12:30am on the 29th of December. Bedwell stated that he had met the two girls and the dark complexioned man in a tavern that morning before they went to the restaurant. He stated that they went to several saloons afterward and ended up in a movie in the 1400 block of Madison Street. He denied that the girls were the Grimes sisters and that they ditched the two men after excusing themselves to the washroom.

Chicago's Haunt Detective

Chicago Ghosts (The unusual suspects)

An operator at The Sunny Lane drive-in restaurant at 5444 Harlem Avenue in Stickney, Casey Jarzen, said that Bedwell was there with the two girls and the man with the dark complexion on January 11th. The story was confirmed by his wife, Mary, a daughter, Donna, and a porter, Chester Wiziecki. All identified the Grimes sisters from photos. The porter, Wiziecki, mentioned that the one girl in the black jacket had the name "Pat" embroidered in the collar of the jacket. Mrs. Grimes failed to mention that fact when she first described what the girls were wearing but confirmed that she indeed had the name "Pat" embroidered in white on the collar of her jacket!

The girls had also been reported on Madison Street by several other persons as well. Robert Hilpertshauser, the manager of the American Theatre at 8 N. Ashland, stated that the girls had been at various movies there from January 5th to January 10th. Edward Martel, a night clerk for a hotel at 1521 Warren Boulevard reported that he saw Barbara leaving with a man coming from a restaurant at 1540 Madison Street.

Sheriff Lohman confirmed that Bedwell admitted the conversation with Duros about the fact that he should let the girls go but refused to give much other information to investigators.

Meanwhile, the autopsy of the Grimes sisters was taking place. Dr. Jerry Kearns, chief pathologist at St. Elizabeth's Hospital and former coroner's pathologist, Dr. Edwin Hirsch, chief pathologist at St. Luke's Hospital, and Dr. A.C. Webb, coroner's pathologist conducted the examination of the bodies. Dr. Walter J.R. Camp, state police toxicologist and professor of toxicology at the University of Illinois, conducted tests on blood and tissue samples. The results of the autopsy only confirmed the mystery. They found that the girls were both virgins and were not sexually molested. The fact that they were found nude was attributed to the fact that the perpetrator(s) were attempting to destroy possible evidence against them. There was no evidence of any exterior violence that would have been capable of causing death. The three puncture wounds observed on Patricia at the scene of the discovery ended up as superficial wounds barely three-quarters of an inch deep. They were not strangled and did not die of carbon monoxide poisoning. There was also evidence of rodent bites and the fact that the bodies had been cold for some time due to the condition of preservation. Barbara's stomach showed that she had eaten roughly three to six hours before she died but they would not hazard a guess as to the date of death.

The FBI released information regarding nine ransom notes that

Friends of the Grimes girls, Dannielle Blotteaux and Barbara Drzewiecki, pose for a photo dressed similarly to the way Barbara and Patricia Grimes were dressed the night they disappeared. *Author's personal collection.*

Mrs. Grimes had received during the search for the girls. They had kept that information confidential in order to protect the safety of the sisters. Eight of the letters were traced to a mental patient in a veteran's hospital. The eight letters, mailed from North Chicago, demanded $1,000 for the safe return of Barbara and Patricia and required Mrs. Grimes, protected by the FBI, to make a trip to Milwaukee, Wisconsin. The letters instructed her to visit a church, a department store, and a place near a downtown hotel at 11am and at 11pm on January 12th. Nobody had ever appeared. Prosecutors declined to prosecute the veteran due to his mental condition.

The ninth letter, which Mrs. Grimes received roughly a week before the girls' bodies were discovered, demanded $5,000 and that it be in $5, $10 and $20 bills. The block print lettering in the note was compared to the writing of Walter Kranz and the FBI deemed the writing "similar."

An unprecedented cooperative team of law enforcement officials was being assembled. Police departments at all levels, federal, state and local, have a reputation of being uncooperative during large investigations due to a number of reasons including, but not unfortunately limited to, the issue of egos. Investigators did not want that occurring in this investigation especially due to the location of the bodies being within a couple hundred feet of the border between Cook County and Du Page County. The agencies agreeing to a "unified command approach" included The Federal Bureau of Investigation, Illinois State Police, Cook and Du Page County Sheriff's departments, Chicago Police Department, Cook County Coroner's Office, the Cook County State's Attorney's Office and the Forest Preserve District Rangers. As mentioned, over 200 officers would eventually comb the area surrounding where the girls were found and the Santa Fe Park area looking for possible clues. A January 25th Chicago Tribune article posted a photo of two friends of the girls', Danielle Blotteaux and Barbara Drzewiecki, dressed in similar clothing as that worn by the Grimes sisters in hopes of locating the missing clothing.

Meanwhile the community of the "Back of the Yards" neighborhood was coming together to raise money for the family to help offset funeral expenses. The funeral services were held at St. Maurice's Church and officiated by the Reverend Joseph Schomburg, whom the family had leaned heavily during the entire ordeal. The funeral services were donated by the Wollschlager Funeral Chapel at 3604 S. Hoyne. The Back of The Yards Council purchased new clothing for the family members. Close to $25,000 was raised by the council, the parish, school, and neighborhood friends. A $20,000 reward was offered for information leading to the arrest and conviction of the killer or killers. A seven-year-old-boy was pictured in a Chicago Tribune article dated January 25, 1957, holding a jar containing $6.08 that he had personally collected.

 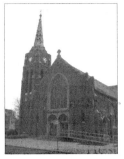

Wollschlager Funeral Home at 3604 S. Hoyne, Chicago, IL. The Wollschlagers donated the cost of the service to the Grimes family.

St. Maurice Church where mass for the girls was attended by thousands including Mayor Richard J. Daley.

The wake and funeral were well attended. Thousands came to pay their respects including Mayor Richard J. Daley himself. A number of times Mrs. Grimes collapsed and sobbed that she was finally with her girls again. Two white closed caskets were each topped with a photo of the young girl whose life was so tragically cut short. The girls were adorned with moonstone rosaries which were blessed by Pope Pius XII and donated by the mother superior of the Poor Clare Order on Laflin Street. Mrs. Grimes put her faith in her God and actually prayed for forgiveness of the monster or monsters who took her girls' lives.

She also made no attempt to disguise her disdain for the way in which the investigation was being handled and for the weeks that she had to convince the authorities that her girls were not runaways. She had told newspapers that the police were not looking for her daughters if they were searching skid row taverns and hotels. She stated, "Leave the killer to God." The girls were laid to rest on January 28, 1957, at Holy Sepulchre Cemetery in Alsip, Illinois, about ten feet from Leona Freck who was another sister who had died two years earlier.

Investigators, however, would see no rest.

It was a huge task. Witnesses had to be re-interviewed, including all of those who had claimed to have seen the girls alive at theatres, restaurants, service stations, bus stops, and train stations. Officers attempted to try to locate the scene of the murder since the popular theory was that the girls were killed in one place and transferred to the location where the bodies were found.

Chicago's Haunt Detective

Chicago Ghosts (The unusual suspects)

Grave marker of Barbara and Patricia Grimes.

Police searched an abandoned farm house that was just west of Wolf Road at 77th Street and found a pile of ashes including some burned clothing in the basement. They also found an abandoned oil truck, in Santa Fe Park with a stain on the seat. It was being examined to determine if the stain could be blood. Twenty-five plastic containers of evidence filled the Chicago police crime laboratory. Articles recovered included bobby pins, glass chips, a lipstick tube, beer cans, cigarette butts, a few rags, a toy sheriff's badge and rings of keys. Two blouses, a belt, and a sweater were also found in the basement of an abandoned dance pavilion in Santa Fe Park but Mrs. Grimes did not recognize them as belonging to the girls'.

Chicago didn't know it yet, but the "Grimes Girls" case was about to take some radical twists and turns. Richard C. Whittenmire, another skid row resident was arrested in the case because he told a Cicero waitress that he knew Bennie Bedwell. The police searched his apartment and found out that shortly after Bedwell's arrest, he had made a phone call to his mother, Elizabeth Whittenmire, a nurse in Mansfield, Ohio. Whittenmire admitted to police that he knew Bedwell and that Bedwell had asked him to go out with two girls once, but he refused. The police found in his hotel room a calendar from the D&L Restaurant and an unmailed letter to his mother in which he wrote, "...went out with a friend last weekend and I am sorry I did." Names and phone numbers were on the calendar and one of those numbers was Bedwell's.

It was beginning to look like they had their man, but two young Ottawa Indian girls came forward to claim that it was they that Bennie had been seen with and not the Grimes sisters. Irene Dean, 19, of 1230 Madison Street, claimed that she and her cousin, Carol King, 18 of Petoskey, Michigan, were with Bedwell and another man at a Madison Street restaurant and theatre.

Meanwhile after three days of intense interrogation, Bennie Bedwell confessed, retracted, and then confessed again in writing that he had killed the Grimes girls along with a man that he had met with the girls at a tavern as "Frank." He stated that this Frank was about 25-26 years old, medium build, 5"9", 150 pounds with light brown wavy hair. He was wearing a tan sport shirt, cream pants, and a gray overcoat. He drove a light blue 1953 Chevy with 1956 South Dakota plates. Bedwell stated that "Frank" worked as a salesperson for a photo company selling coupon books. The following is a summary of Bennie Bedwell's first statement to police:

> Bedwell stated that he met the two girls and a man by the name of "Frank" at Harold's Club Tavern on the corner of Madison and Loomis Streets on the 7th of January between 7:30am and 8:30am. He offered to buy the "bigger one" a drink but the bartender wouldn't serve them. They decided to go to the Greenfont Tavern, which was four doors west of Harold's, and had between six to eight rounds of drinks. They then left there and went to the D&L Restaurant to eat and drink coffee. After they left the D&L, they went back to the Greenfont and had another three to six rounds. After that, they went to another bar on the corner of Madison and Loomis (he couldn't recall the name), and had another three drinks. After that, they went to a theatre three doors west of the bar and the girls excused themselves to go to the restroom and ran out on them. He said that Frank wanted to go after them but he wanted to stay and watch the movie since they already paid for it. He then said that three days later he saw "the big one" at The Jackpot Tavern on the 900 block of Madison Street but she wouldn't talk to him. He then stated that the following day the same girl came into the bakery that he worked at and refused to speak with him again. He said that he never saw the girls again after that.

Bennie soon retracted that statement after the continued interrogation. Sheriff Lohman took him, along with other police personnel to the Caffarello's motel at 55th and Cicero Avenue. The motel was owned by one of Sheriff Lohman's men. At 12:10am on the 27th of January, they called State's Attorney Adamowski and a clerk into the room to take Bedwell's new and revised statement. In the room was Sheriff Lohman, Undersheriff Brennan, Chief Dreyer, Captain Fleming, Sergeant Hederman, Chief Investigator Anheier, Cook County State's Attorney Benjamin S. Adamowski and a clerk.

The statement was tape recorded and typed. Bennie Bedwell could not read or write except for writing his name.

Chicago Ghosts (The unusual suspects)

Bennie stated that he was working at a Bakery at 949 W. Madison Street in the same building as the hotel in which he lived. He had worked in the bakery for about two weeks and, before that, was employed at Ajax Consolidated at 4615 W. 20th Street. Adamowski asked him if he understood his rights and knew that his statement was being recorded and he stated that he did. He asked him if he was threatened by the police and he said that he wasn't. Adamowski asked him if he promised any leniency based on his statement and he said, "Break that down into English." Adamowski asked him if the police had promised to go easy on him if he made a statement and he said that they hadn't. Bennie stated that he met the two girls who were already with a guy named Frank at Harold's Club on the 1300 block on W. Madison. They then went to the Crest Hotel and registered under assumed names but he doesn't remember what name he registered as. He stated that Frank slept with Barbara and he slept with Patricia. He stated that the sexual acts were twice the next morning and then they went out to eat and came back to the Crest Hotel that night and went drinking the next day. He stated that on January 9th he and Patricia went to Lorraine's house (Lorraine was a colored woman who lives on the 1200 block of Washington). He didn't know where Frank and the other girl had gone. On the 10th, they went to the west end and got a room for the day at 19 N. Racine. They stayed for two nights for free because Bennie was broke. On the 12th, they had to leave and registered at the West End Hotel as Mr. and Mrs. Smith and Frank and Barbara were at 19 N. Racine. On Sunday the 13th, the four walked up and down Madison Street and went to the Aberdeen bar after noon. Frank left for about 1½ hours and the girl and he stayed at the bar drinking beer and gin.

Frank came back with a light blue 1953 Chevrolet. Bedwell didn't know where he'd gotten it and thought it could have been stolen. They went for a ride and had some hot dogs at a restaurant. They then went to a service station where the girls had to use the bathroom. He couldn't say whether or not the girls went into the station or used the outdoors. After they left there, they took the girls to a forest preserve to have sex but the girls resisted them. Bedwell stated that he accidentally hit Patricia too hard on the chin and knocked her out. He could hear Frank and Barbara scuffling and suddenly the scuffling stopped so Bedwell assumed that Frank had knocked Barbara out. They panicked and drove the girls to where they had found the bodies. He stated that they stripped the clothing off to hide fingerprints and that *he dropped Patricia over the guard rail about 200 feet east of County Line Road on German Church Road. He then pulled Barbara out of the car and dropped her over the guard rail as well. Adamowski asked Bedwell how the bodies were lying and he stated that he believes that Barbara's head was under Patricia. (which actually did not make any sense if he dropped Barbara over the guard rail after Patricia. Patricia was found on top of Barbara.) After that, they took off on Route 66 and Ogden Avenue and drove back to Madison Street. Frank stated that he would dispose of the clothes and left.*

The next day, January 28, 1957, was a media circus. The sheriff and the deputies who "cracked the case" were in the newspapers and they were taking Bedwell out to recreate it.

They started at the Sheriff's special investigations office which was a converted store front with large windows at 6204 Archer Avenue. There were over 100 people attempting to catch a glance of Bedwell. They rushed Bedwell from the building into a waiting Cadillac. Bedwell was in fear for his life from the sneering crowd.

The first stop was The Sunny Lane drive-in restaurant at 5444 S. Harlem where the girls had eaten hot dogs before they died. This time there were over 500 people and they pushed through the crowd to the inside of the restaurant. Bedwell was seen chewing gum nervously.

They scurried back into the vehicle and drove to the gas station at Archer and Willow Springs Road where the girls had used the bathroom. There were only about 200 people there, but Bedwell did not get out of the car. The crowd was not happy with that.

The third stop was the roadside park at Willow Springs Road and 87th Street where the girls were rendered unconscious. Again, Bedwell did not get out of the vehicle.

The fourth and final stop was at the infamous drop spot near German Church Road and County Line Road. The lines of cars seemed to go on for miles. Law enforcement, press, and curiosity seekers lined both sides of the road and over 50 policeman could not hold the pressing crowds back. Bedwell got out of the vehicle and demonstrated how he pulled Patricia out of the vehicle and then went back for Barbara. It seemed that the Grimes case was finally over, but soon things started falling apart for Sheriff Lohman's case.

The Chicago Tribune located "Frank." Frank was actually a man by the name of William Cole Willingham and he was serving a thirty-day sentence in the Brideswell for disorderly conduct. He was a Virginian who called himself the "hillbilly singer." He was another resident of skid row and had worked as a salesman for the Hoffman Photo Studio at 305 E. Adams. Harry Cohen who owned the studio fired Willingham back in November of 1956. It seemed that Willingham admitted knowing Bedwell and stated that he had been with Bedwell at the D&L Restaurant and movie theatre with two Indian girls—not the Grimes Sisters. He was also working at a drug store at Grand Avenue and Clark Street on January 7, when Bedwell said he met him at Harold's. This was confirmed by

Bennie Bedwell (in center with hand outstretched) shows where he dumped the bodies of the Grimes sisters along German Church Road. Sheriff Lohman is to his right. *Author's personal collection.*

Willingham's employer. Additionally, he was working at a drug store at 4761 N. Broadway on the 11th and 12th when he and Barbara were supposed to be staying at 19 N. Racine. This was also confirmed.

The coroner's inquest did not go much better for Sheriff Lohman. Mrs. Grimes was there and was actually comforting Bedwell's mother who was also there. She told her that she didn't believe that her son committed the crimes. Dr. Camp's toxicology and tissue results were back and it seemed that the contents of Barbara's stomach were the same as what she had during her last meal at home before the fateful movie night of December 28, 1956. That would mean that they would have to have been killed between four to six hours from the time that they ate or roughly very soon after the movie ended. That fact alone discredited Bedwell's statement about killing the girls on the 13th of January. Patricia's stomach was empty but Mrs. Grimes had already said that Patricia had not eaten nearly as much as Barbara had. There was also no evidence of any alcohol consumption by either of the girls. When Coroner Walter McCarron asked Dr. Walter J.R. Camp whether or not either girl was sexually molested, Dr. Camp refused to answer the question because it was a question of morality. Mrs. Grimes looked right at Bedwell and asked him, "Why are you lying?" Other factors concerning Bedwell's statement were also starting to fall apart. The porter from the restaurant where the girls allegedly ate had mentioned that the letters PAT were sewn into the one girl's collar. Mrs. Grimes confirmed this but later found out the Patricia had removed the patch three days before she had seen the movie on December 28th. Also, Bedwell had mentioned signing into several hotels under different names and he was illiterate except for being after to write his name. Investigators were also unable to produce any hotel registers with any of the names that Bedwell had said that he signed in as.

Bedwell now had an attorney named David Bradshaw who was moving to have Bedwell released as a result of this new information. Bradshaw also noticed that Bedwell had an injury to the inside of his bottom lip.

Bedwell later recanted his signed and tape-recorded confession. He testified before Chief Justice Wilbert F. Crowley of the Criminal Court at a hearing on a writ of habeas corpus obtained by his attorney. Bedwell alleged that he was beaten and threatened by Cook County Sheriff's Chief Clifford Dreyer. He stated that Dreyer hit him in the lip, and the head behind the ear. He also stated that Dreyer kicked him and twirled the cylinder of a revolver as Bedwell was being questioned. He also threatened to bring a "Blackjack" back into the room with him and Bedwell would not like that. Bedwell said that he had been deprived of food and sleep for three days and just confessed in order to cease the torture. He said that all he did was substitute the Grimes sister for the two Indian girls that he had gone out with and then just retold the story of killing the sisters based on what he had been reading in the newspaper.

Bedwell was eventually released on bond and Sheriff Lohman came under fire from the Civil Liberties Union for holding Bedwell for over ninety hours without formal charges. The Coroner's jury came back with a finding of murder but the only cause of death was exposure to the elements. They found no reason to investigate Bedwell any further. Walter Kranz had been cleared for some time and it seemed that the investigators were back to square one.

In February 1957, the police followed up with a couple weak leads including arresting a 16-year-old gang member named Richard Byrnes. Byrnes, according to Mrs. Grimes, took much joy in picking on Barbara and had thrown her shoe in a McKinley Park pond. They had picked up Byrnes and a couple of his other juvenile gang members who were currently on bond for beating a sailor who was home on leave and one of the sailor's friends. They were later cleared of any wrongdoing in the Grimes case.

In April, a man named Frederick Dyer, 48, of 150 Eugenie Street, was arrested on rape charges and "lie tested" on both the rape and the Grimes case and was cleared of any wrongdoing.

In May of the same year, Mrs. Grimes received an anonymous phone call from a male caller claiming to know who killed her girls. He stated that he was there and helped to undress them. "I know something about your little girl that no one else knows but you—not even the police," the caller said. "It's never been in the papers. The smallest girl's toes were crossed on both of her feet." After that the caller laughed cruelly and hung up. The family had also received phone calls from callers who would just breathe heavily and hang up.

It seemed like there could have been a break in the case, when the beaten body of Mary Lou Wagner, 14, was fished out of an ice-filled pond just north of Glenview Naval Air Station. She was fully clothed and the only things missing were her shoes and a purse. Robert Max

Fleig, 17, a recent inmate at the Illinois State Training School for Boys in Kane County and Sheridan reformatory, was questioned by investigators once and released. A citizen had then reported finding the victim's wallet on the street over the weekend and the police thought the wallet looked as though someone had been holding the wallet because it appeared very clean.

They recalled Fleig and he was in the offices of John Reid waiting to take a voluntary lie detector test when he admitted to killing Wagner. He stated that he just recently met Wagner and picked her up at Dewey's Coffee Shop at 6404 N. Clark Street. He drove her to the area near the pond because it was more or less a "lovers lane" type area. After she refused his sexual advances, he strangled her and beat her with a rolling pin that he had because he worked at his father's bakery at 6621 N. Clark Street. Fleig led Detectives Arthur Bilek and John O'Grady of the Rogers Park station and Captain James Hackett, deputy chief of the uniform police, to the pond which was half a mile north of the Willow Road overpass north of the air station. Fleig was given a lie detector with regard to the Grimes case and the results were promising. The problem was that originally when given the test the investigators were told that Fleig was 18 when he was actually 17, or a juvenile, which made the administration of the test unlawful and inadmissible.

Fleig eventually plead guilty to the murder as well as admitting to several beatings of females and one Rogers Park rape. He was sentenced to life in prison. On Mother's Day in 1959, Robert M. Fleig's mother, Margaret Fleig, 45, of 6621 N. Clark tried to commit suicide by taking an overdose of sleeping pills. Her attempt at killing herself because of her son's life sentence was unsuccessful and ended up merely making her ill. Her husband, Max, said that she was in better spirits toward the middle of the week and he took their other children to a movie. The next morning, Sunday, at 5:30am, Max discovered his wife lying in a pool of blood on the living room floor. She had shot herself in the head and the German Luger pistol lay by her side. Fleig had never been further questioned or charged in the Grimes case and learned of his mother's death from a radio broadcast that he was listening to from the Joliet State Penitentiary.

The case had gone cold. Mrs. Grimes was working as a matron at the police Bridewell helping with female prisoners. Bennie Bedwell swore that he would turn over a new leaf but faced rape charges in Florida which he eventually beat. He returned to skid row in Chicago and worked for a while with the Salvation Army. I had read in a couple of web articles that Bennie had been imprisoned on weapons charges and released in 1986, but I tend to believe that information to be false because I had discovered that Edward Lee (Bennie) Bedwell had died on November 25, 1972 at the young age of 37 and was buried on November 29, 1972 at the Jefferson Barracks National Cemetery, St. Louis, Missouri. The authorities promised Mrs. Grimes that they would never give up on the case and it still remains open to this day. Mr. Grimes died in 1989 at the age of 83 and is buried in the same cemetery as Patricia and Barbara.

For many years investigator's believed that the Schuessler and Peterson murders of 1955 were in some way related to the Grimes murders because both cases were unsolved, and in both cases the victims were young and found nude in wooded areas. Almost forty years after finding the bodies of Robert Peterson, 14, and brothers

Grave marker of the girls' mother, Loretta Grimes.

John, 13, and Anton Schuessler Jr., 11, investigators from the Bureau of Alcohol Tobacco and Firearms were investigating the 1977 disappearance of millionaire, heiress Helen Vorhees Brach when an informant provided information on the murder.

Sometimes it is much better to be lucky than good. Based on information from the 1994 investigation, police arrested Kenneth Hansen, 61. Hansen was a stable hand employed by horseman, Silas Jayne. At the time of the murders, Hansen was a strong 22 year old. Police said that he found the boys hitchhiking down Milwaukee Avenue south of Lawrence Avenue. The boys had been out for a day at the movies and bowling alleys. Hansen lured them into the car and drove them to the Idle Hour Stable which was owned by Jayne. While there, he tried to pay the boys to perform sexual acts and when the boys resisted he became angry and strangled them. Jayne learned of the killings and was furious with Hansen. It is believed that Jayne helped Hansen dispose of the bodies in a ditch at the Robinson Woods Forest Preserve. In May of 1956, shortly after investigators had announced that they were going to exhume the boys bodies to look for further physical evidence, Hansen set fire to the barn burning it to the ground. Hay was found in the boys' lungs. Jayne filed an insurance claim on the barn. In 1971, Jayne was charged with ordering the murder of his brother, George, and Hansen was indicted on the same charge. Jayne was convicted, served time in prison, and died in 1986. Hansen was never convicted.

Hansen went on to get married and have children. He and his wife opened Camelot Stable in the 1960s and operated it until they sold it in the late 1980s. It came out in Hansen's trials (he was re-tried in 2002) that he had molested hundreds of young boys over the years. Four Federal informants testified that Hansen had confessed to the murders to them at least twelve times. He was convicted twice and sentenced to 200 years. He was not eligible for the death penalty because of a loophole that allows people who are convicted many years after a crime to choose the year that they wish to be sentenced under, and his defense chose a year in which Illinois did not have a death penalty.

Ghostly Vehicle

While one horrendous crime had closure, there was no such luck with the Grimes case. It is no wonder that there have been reports of ghostly activity near the site where the Grimes sisters were found. As I had mentioned before, the horror is still very fresh in the minds of those who had experienced the case first-hand. Many of those persons were the same age as the sisters when they were murdered.

They call it the ghost car of old German Church Road. There are numerous reports of persons who find themselves along that lonely stretch of road just on the Cook County side of the Du Page / Cook County line. The sound of a vehicle pulling off to the side of the road, a door opening, the sound of heavy thuds, door closing, and a vehicle speeding off into the distance.

I had the opportunity to hear Robert Miller, a local Chicago folklorist, speak during a paranormal tour that took place on the 53rd anniversary of the discovery of the Grimes sisters. He was a guest tour guide on one of Ursula Bielski's Chicago Hauntings Ghost Tours. He remembers going to the area as a juvenile with his friends. There used to be an abandoned house near the area where the Grimes sisters were found. The legend is that the house was quickly abandoned after the Grimes sisters were discovered a short distance away on the side of the road near Devil's Creek. One story is that the residents of the house started experiencing hauntings shortly after and left the

Chicago's Haunt Detective

Chained gate and No Trespass sign at 8275 County Line Road, Hinsdale, IL where a house was quickly abandoned after the murders and ghost cars have been seen.

area so quickly that they left dishes on the table and many personal possessions in the house, including a 1955 Buick in the garage. The other story is that a couple lived there and the wife lost her mind shortly after the discovery of the murder victims. The wife remained in the house and the husband moved. Mr. Miller did verify that the house was there when he visited there as a kid with his friends and they peered into the windows. He did say that it still looked as though many possessions were still in the house, although it had been pretty well damaged by time and vandalized. He also confirmed the rusted hulk of a vehicle in the garage.

I had come across a story on http://www.prairieghosts.com entitled "Farewell to the Grimes Sisters" by Troy Taylor. Mr. Taylor is a local author and also runs a tour called Haunted America Tours. In the article, he mentions a story told by another author, Tamara Shaffer. According to the article, a young woman was leading a group on a tour of the house and site one evening when they witnessed a dark vehicle with no lights pull up the driveway, circle the house, speed past them and then

Remains of the house at 8275 County Line Road.

disappear. They decided to leave and encountered a police officer who had been sent there to chase off the tour group. The chain that stretched across the driveway was still intact and the officer claimed that he had seen no other cars.

I decided to take a visit to the site and have to admit that one gets a very sad, lonely feeling at the location. The area where the house stood is private property and marked with *No Trespass* signs. The old white wooden gate is still intact and chained. There is evidence of a house that stood at one point and the only building left standing is what appears to be an old wooden outhouse. The vacant land is surrounding by some of

Inside of the bath house at 8275 County Line Road.

the most beautiful new houses in very affluent subdivisions but for some reason the land nearest where the Grimes sisters were found is strangely undeveloped.

If you walk north, past where the house used to stand, there is what looks like a hand-built stone structure resembling the shape of a rounded cave. It has a fireplace and windows and looks like a very well-built little stone house. It appears that it is well used due to the number of empty beer cans that I found there as well as some homemade smoking materials and the remains of a fairly recent fire. The old mailbox from the address was crudely inserted into the ground near the structure and simply read "8275." I had remembered seeing the fireplace in a photo of a 1957 *Chicago Tribune* article that chronicled the search efforts. It showed an investigator sifting through the fireplace and the caption referred to the place as a grotto located on private property. I decided to see if I could find any information on the owners of the property at the time of the Grimes killings.

Outside of the cave-like grotto on the County Line property.

What I did find is that the ten acres where the abandoned house at 8275 County Line Road stood was part of a larger area of land owned by the John Fischer Family since at least 1873. I found that the ten acres in question were sold by Leona Fischer, the widow of Herman Fischer and descendants of John Fischer, to George and Beatrice Tinsley on September 18, 1950, for $70,000. The couple was from Glen Ellyn, Illinois. George was 60 years old at the time and his wife, Beatrice, was 50 years old. I could not find a transfer of that property or mention of the Tinsley name in land records from the 1950s, 60s or 70s, so I don't believe that there was a quick transfer of property after the Grimes killings. That doesn't mean that whoever was living there at the time didn't move quickly, it just means the property wasn't sold during that time. George Tinsley passed away in 1974 in Palm Beach, Florida, as did his wife, Beatrice, in 1994. The property is currently privately owned purchased from a bank in the 1980s and is still undeveloped.

The Grimes case still remains unsolved.

Inside of the grotto with a view of the fireplace which was searched following the Grimes murders.

The Guardian Angel Spirit Church
(A Case of Bad Karma or Pure Evil?)

This particular case hits pretty close to home. The tragic end result of the happenings on 28th Place in Chicago ended in the death of a young law enforcement professional. I agonized over whether or not to include this case in the book because I didn't want readers to interpret the inclusion as being a glamorization of the circumstances that resulted in the death of a fellow officer. The inclusion is also not meant to give notoriety to the individuals responsible, but hopefully is more of a testimony to the dangers that officers face every day and their heroic actions that enable us to live in relative safety.

Many times you will hear people say that you shouldn't mess with things like séances or Ouija boards because you never know what type of spirits or evil you could possibly unleash. You may or not believe the warning but this case may be one of those situations. At the very least, it seems that it could be a severe example of "Murphy's Law" – whatever could go wrong, will go wrong. Leave it to the Irish to be so optimistic.

John Annerino Jr. was born in Chicago on May 21, 1930, to John Annerino Sr. and Mamie La Rocco. Annerino was many things to many people. One of his personas was as the dumpy, disheveled looking, Chicago city employee. Annerino had begun his career in Chicago politics and government as a loyal member of the legendary 11th Ward Democratic machine headed up by Mayor Richard J. Daley. He had also been a long-time police precinct captain, although he had resigned from that position in the early 1980s. His last position in city government was that of the director of administration for the Chicago city clerk's office. On the surface, he seemed like a

Chicago City Hall where John Annerino worked.

dedicated, fairly quiet, career city government guy. What most people didn't realize is that he had a completely different life outside of the walls of city hall.

When he wasn't at his day job, Annerino was the self-styled minister and spiritual healer for his church, The Guardian Angel Spirit Church, that he ran out of the basement of his home in the 500 block of West 28th place. It was said that he held séances and spiritual healing sessions on a regular basis. In August of 1984, Annerino was in a bar called "Halsted's" when he met 37-year-old, Robert Fischer. Fischer was working as a security guard at a bar called "The Loading Dock" which was just next door. They struck up a conversation and Annerino told Fischer that he wanted to start up a bar someday but couldn't because it would be considered a conflict of interest with his position as a city employee. Annerino proposed that Fischer could act as a "front" for the bar and Fischer agreed that it could work. At some point in the evening, Annerino told Fischer that he was the minister of "The Guardian Angel Spiritual Independent Church" that he ran out of his basement at 515 W. 28th Place. (At this point in the conversation is where most people would run for the door but that wouldn't make much of a story now would it?)

Fischer's reply to that statement was that he too was a minister! Annerino was elated and offered Fischer the position of senior pastor in

John Annerino's house and site of séances during services of The Guardian Angel Spirit Church.

the church because he was looking to retire in the near future. There was a catch, however. A condition of being the senior pastor in the church required that Fischer live in Annerino's house. (Now, who could turn down an offer like that? Okay...okay, I promise to keep the sarcasm at a minimum.) After Fischer moved in, Annerino placed Fischer's name on several bank accounts, and in January, 1985, he arranged for Fischer to start work as a license examiner in the Chicago City Clerk's Office. Annerino also purchased a Lincoln Continental in the name of the church for Fischer to use.

I had contacted the Illinois Attorney General's Office and the Illinois Secretary of State's Office regarding The Guardian Angel Spiritual Independent Church. An organization would have to register with both offices if it were operating as a church with a church non-profit status and neither office had any records of the church ever existing. I did however find an article in *The Chicago Tribune* dated January 3, 1982, entitled, "Abuse of charity license plates seen." The article touted how luxury vehicles were being outfitted with special charity license plates at $4 per year rather than the $18 or $30 that regular license plates cost in 1982. The Guardian Angel Spiritual Church was listed as one of the potential abusers of the system with charity license plates adorning a 1981 Cadillac. I find it very interesting, but definitely not surprising, that a city employee with an unregistered, supposedly non-profit organization, can somehow end up with charity license plates issued by the same organization that they were never registered with.

Fischer soon found out that strange things were going on in the church. The "services" were actually séances held in the basement of the home by Annerino in an attempt to contact spirits of the dearly departed of members of the church. If that wasn't enough, the "church" also doubled as a workout area and oil-wrestling arena for local male body-building enthusiasts. I am not sure what church Fischer claimed to be a minister of before he met Annerino, but I am guessing that Annerino's church was one-of-a-kind.

According to court documents, Annerino made sexual advances toward Fischer between February and May of 1985. Fischer had brushed off the advances which angered Annerino. Fischer called his mother on Mother's Day, May 11, 1985, and following that phone call, Annerino became enraged. He had accused Fischer of having received a message from his mother about a woman that Annerino had suspected Fischer of having a relationship with. Fischer countered by telling Annerino that he was leaving the church. At this point, Annerino lost his mind and screamed at Fischer and told him that being a pastor in the church was a lifetime commitment and that the only way he could leave the church was in a casket! Annerino threatened to "stomp on him like a cockroach" if he left the church. Fischer cut his ties with Annerino and The Guardian Angel Spiritual Church on June 30, 1985 and moved back into his family's residence on Maple Street in Prospect Heights, a northwest suburb of Chicago.

Fischer returned to his job at the city clerk's office the next day and, as Fischer was probably expecting, Annerino informed him that he was fired. Fischer defiantly told Annerino that Annerino did not have the authority to fire him and that only Walter Kozubowski, the city clerk, could fire him. Annerino, much like an enraged juvenile, ran into Kozubowski's office and within five minutes, Kozubowski called Fischer into his office and informed him that he was being terminated because of poor job performance. One might assume that having Fischer fired would be enough but it was only the beginning. The normally quiet dedicated city worker was now on a mission to make Fischer's life a living hell or worse.

On August 2, 1985 at about 5am, Fischer's mother was awakened to the sound of a brick shattering her living room window. The Fischer family contacted the police and Cook County Sheriff's Police Officer Dean Endre responded to the call. At 5:58am, Fischer received a phone call and as luck would have it, Officer Endre was still there and listened in. They heard a male caller state, "Did you see what happened earlier, Bobby? Your whole f***ing world is about to come to an end."

On August 12, 1985, Fischer was served with papers. Annerino had filed a lawsuit alleging that Fischer owned him $35,000 in return for the 6 months of room and board and storage that Annerino provided him. In response, Fischer filed a countersuit demanding the return of his possessions.

Then on October 5, 1985, things took a deadly turn. Fischer was on his way home from his job as a security guard at "Christopher Street," a bar on Halsted Street in Chicago. An unknown assailant shot at Fischer while he was in his vehicle. The assailant had seemingly missed. Fischer was unharmed but later discovered that a bullet had lodged in the seat belt that he was wearing. The seat belt had more than likely saved his life, but not in the way that it was designed to! Fischer reported the incident to the Chicago Police.

Chicago's Haunt Detective

Allen Falls Jr. was 22 years old and lived on Wentworth on Chicago's south side. He'd known Annerino since he was 12 years old through his uncle. His uncle suggested that he should go in to talk to Annerino about getting a city job. On October 13, 1985, Falls, his cousin, Ira Jackson, 23 and Falls' uncle went to Annerino's house. Annerino stated that all they had to do was apply for jobs down at City Hall and give him the serial numbers of the applications. Annerino promised them that they would have jobs by the end of the week. Before they left, Annerino asked them if they could return the favor and help him with a problem that he was having. According to Falls, Annerino claimed that an ex-employee named Robert Fischer had been harassing him and that Fischer was trying to intimidate him. Ira Jackson later told investigators that Annerino had offered them increasing amounts of money to kill Fischer. He started at $3,000 and then $6,000 and then finally $9,000 to have Fischer killed. Falls and Jackson said that they had an associate, Dwayne Coulter, who was a security guard and had access to firearms. Annerino allegedly accompanied Falls and Jackson to Fischer's house in Prospect Heights and showed them a picture of Fischer.

Dwayne Coulter was a 27-year-old who, by all accounts, was an individual with anger issues. He was born to Leslie Coulter and Earnestine Welsch on August 1, 1958, in Chicago. His father was a hard worker and had purchased their first home at 10924 South Indiana Street after twelve years in the Cabrini Green Housing Projects. Coulter had five brothers and sisters and got average grades in School. In 1976, he was evaluated psychologically because of poor school attendance and grade performance at the request of the school system. He spent two months in an in-patient treatment center. Coulter dropped out of high school and joined the U.S. Army Reserves as an Infantryman in 1976. He served some active duty time in 1978 with Co. A, 1st Battalion, 11th Infantry at Ft. Carson, Colorado. He had a way of finding his way into trouble and received a demotion for threatening violence against one of his superiors. He eventually went AWOL in 1979, and never returned to the military. His mother died of Pancreatic Cancer in 1978, and according to statements by family members, Coulter became more angry and depressed. He did finish training as a security guard and completed a thirty-hour program in security and firearms training at the American Security Training Institute. In March of 1979, he received a certificate qualifying him to carry firearms from the Illinois Department of Registration and Education.

He had a spotty criminal record as well. He was arrested in 1977 for criminal trespass and theft of services, in 1983 for criminal damage and in May of 1985 for robbery.

It is unclear what type of financial agreement Falls, Jackson and Coulter had, but it seemed clear that they were going to find a couple of patsies to actually do the dirty work at a fraction of what they were going to be paid by Annerino.

Bobby Lindsey was approached by Falls and Jackson on October 14th about killing Robert Fischer for an unspecified amount of money. Lindsey stated later that he was told that they wanted him dead because Fischer had stolen cocaine from them. On October 15th Lindsey, Falls and Jackson drove to Fischer's house in Prospect Heights. Falls gave Lindsey a .22 caliber pistol and told Lindsey to go to the front door and kill Fischer. Lindsey, who stated that he was having car trouble, was met at the door by Fischer's mother who told Lindsey that Fischer was not at home. The three men left.

Vincent Steven Calvin was also approached by Falls and Jackson and he was offered $2,000 to kill Fischer.

On October 16th, Calvin, Lindsey, Falls, Jackson, and Coulter all traveled to Fischer's house. The story was that if they were stopped by police, they were on their way to Schaumburg to look for jobs. Upon arrival at the Fischer house, Falls gave Calvin a .22 caliber pistol while Coulter gave Lindsey a .357. They were instructed by Falls, Jackson, and Coulter to go to the door and pose as aluminum siding salespeople. When they asked for Fischer at the front door, they were again turned away and told that Fischer was not at home. The five men left the area.

Later that day, Fischer received a phone call from a male claiming to be a Chicago Police Officer. The male stated that he had a warrant for Fischer's arrest because he was two months behind in car payments. The caller advised Fischer to be home at 9:30am the following morning. Fischer was not late on his car payments. He called the Cook County Sheriff's Police, Prospect Heights detail and spoke with Officer Michael Ridges.

The next morning, October 17, 1985, Officer Michael Ridges, who had just been promoted to juvenile officer two weeks earlier due to his love of working with children, arrived at Fischer's residence at 9am. Officer Ridges spoke with Fischer for about ten minutes, wrote a report, and left the residence. Within minutes, Officer Ridges noticed a light blue 1975 Cadillac with no license plates about one block from Fischer's residence. The Cadillac was occupied by Coulter, Falls, and Jackson.

304				
COURT BRANCH	COURT DATE		SHEET	LINE

IN THE CIRCUIT COURT OF COOK COUNTY, ILLINOIS

PEOPLE OF THE STATE OF ILLINOIS
vs.

JOHN ANNERINO

Case No. *85-C-12906* #203 November, 1985 (Grand Jury)

BFW [ ]

ARREST WARRANT

THE PEOPLE OF THE STATE OF ILLINOIS TO ALL PEACE OFFICERS IN THE STATE — GREETING:

We command you to arrest _____ John Annerino _____
(Defendant)

for the offense of _____ 38 _____ 9-1 _____ Murder _____
(Chapter) (Section) (Description)

Stated in a charge now pending before this court and that you bring him instanter before The Circuit Court of Cook County at_____

2600 S. California, Rm. 101, Chicago, Cook County, Illinois
(Location)

or, if I am absent or unable to act, the nearest or most accessible court in Cook County or, if this warrant is executed in a county other than Cook, before the nearest or most accessible judge in the county where the arrest is made.

Issued in Cook County _____ November 6, _____ , 19 85

Arrest warrant for John Annerino.

At 9:21am, Officer Ridges pulled the vehicle over near the intersection of Willow Road and Elmhurst Road (IL Route 83). Ridges was in plain clothes and driving an unmarked police car.

Officer Ridges approached the vehicle and asked Falls, the driver, for his driver's license and to step out of the vehicle. He then asked Jackson for some identification and Jackson replied that he did not have any identification. He then asked Jackson to step out of the vehicle. It is unclear if Ridges had asked Coulter to step out of the vehicle or whether Coulter simply left the vehicle to face off on Ridges. As Coulter exited the vehicle, Ridges noticed that he was wearing a light blue shirt that had an outdated Chicago Police patch on the shoulder. He was also wearing a leather belt and holster. According to court documents, Ridges asked Coulter if he was a police officer and Coulter asked, "What does it look like?" He asked Coulter if he had a weapon, and at some point, Coulter shoved Ridges and drew his gun with both hands. Coulter fired two shots at Ridges. One fatal shot struck Ridges in the head and one shot ricocheted off the ground striking Falls in the leg. The men ran back to the car and fled the area.

Officer Lussky, who heard Officer Ridges call in the original traffic stop requesting backup, also heard the next call minutes later of an officer shot at the same location. Officer Lussky arrived to find Ridges with an injury on his chin and a fatal gunshot wound to the head. He also found Falls' driver's license close to Ridges.

Officer John Kucharski of the Chicago Police Department located the vehicle southbound on the Kennedy Expressway. Kucharski, Officer Dennis Tabaka and Officer Ted Ochocki stopped the vehicle on the Kennedy Expressway near Lawrence Avenue. They conducted a felony traffic stop and ordered the occupants out of the vehicle. Coulter was still wearing the police shirt. Coulter screamed as he exited the vehicle, "I did a bad thing. Shoot me in the head!" A pistol, badge, and police scanner were plainly visible in the vehicle. Officer Tabaka searched Coulter and found a .38 caliber pistol with two spent shells and four intact rounds in the chambers. It was later determined that it was the same gun that killed Officer Ridges. There was also powder residue on Coulter's hands.

Coulter had at one time argued that the gun went off accidentally when he slammed the gun on the back trunk of the car because he was angry at Ridges for not believing that he was a security guard. Test results showed no trace of powder residue on the vehicle itself discrediting Coulter's statement. Also found in Coulter's possession were phone numbers and addresses for Mrs. Fischer as well as Annerino's address and phone number. Officer Kucharski found a .22 caliber revolver and a police star on the front seat. Falls was transported to Northwestern Hospital where he was treated for a very superficial wound which doctors stated would not even need medication. Eventually Falls, Jackson, and Coulter were transported and interrogated. This was not the first time that Coulter was found impersonating a police officer. In 1982, he was arrested for impersonating a police officer but the case was dropped. This time Coulter also had a badge and credentials claiming that he was State Senate Investigator. The credentials bore the signature of State Senator Charles Chew. Chew denied knowing Coulter and also denied issuing any such credentials with his name on it. It did so happen that at that time, politicians rewarded political worker bees with police badges and or credentials as a matter of routine.

During the course of interrogations, the separate defendants told varying versions of the story but generally the stories were similar.

On October 21st, Police conducted a search warrant on Annerino's home and discovered a photo of Fischer, phone numbers of the suspects, large amounts of homosexual pornography, and bank books totaling near $500,000. Annerino stated that he had met Falls, Jackson, and Coulter three weeks prior when they had asked him if they could use his basement as a workout facility. He claimed that he was helping them find jobs and that he had never asked them to kill anyone. He also stated that he would never hurt Mr. Fischer or anyone else.

On the same day, Michael Ridges was being laid to rest at an Oak Lawn Funeral. Attending the funeral were his wife, Sharon; his father, Chicago Lawn Area Captain, John W. Ridges; his brother, Sgt. John W. Ridges Jr. of the Wentworth Area violent crimes unit and 1,000 other law enforcement officers. Sheriff Richard Elrod read a prayer for the slain officer.

On November 6, 1985, the grand jury indicted John Annerino, Dwayne Makia Coulter, Allen Falls Jr., and Ira Jackson on charges of felony murder in the death of Cook County Sheriff's Officer Michael Ridges and on conspiracy to commit the murder of Robert Fischer. The Warrant for Annerino's arrest was issued the same day.

At 7:45pm, just three hours after his indictment, Annerino was leaving a friend's house at 1010 S. Menard, when he was gunned down in front of the residence. Annerino was shot once in the stomach. Even though he was conscious and able to speak to investigators, Annerino said nothing and died three hours later. Robert Fischer was placed in protective custody.

Police thought that Annerino's death could be that he was linked to a cousin, Sam Annerino, who was a prominent crime syndicate figure who was gunned down in 1977. The bullet used to kill Annerino was a round-nosed lead bullet used primarily for target practice and although it appeared to be a classic set-up type hit, he was shot in an uncustomary location. Witnesses said that the assailant appeared to be a white male wearing a plaid shirt and blue jeans.

Police later learned that Annerino was planning to visit a friend named Martha Kay who had attended "services" at The Guardian Angel Spirit Church. He had called her and an individual who was to give him a ride shortly before he was killed. They eventually spoke to a Bridgeport man who was a tire repair shop owner and neighbor of Annerino named William Rubio. Rubio was 30 years old and lived at 2918 S. Union Avenue. Rubio eventually admitted to the fact that he shot and killed Annerino, but there was another bizarre twist. Annerino had wanted Rubio to shoot him! Rubio told police that Annerino had wanted Rubio to shoot him in order to gain sympathy from a prospective jury pool and also to possibly

Annerino grave marker. John Annerino is buried in an unmarked grave in this family plot even though his will stated that he wanted his ashes spread over Lake Michigan.

Building at 1010 S. Menard, Chicago, IL. John Annerino was shot to death on the sidewalk in front of the building.

frame his former roommate, Robert Fischer. Annerino told Rubio that he wanted to be shot in the arm or leg and Rubio talked him out of it. Rubio told him that no one would believe the story if he was shot in the arm or the leg. It had to be the stomach. Rubio said that he never had the intention to kill Annerino. Rubio was eventually charged with involuntary manslaughter and a couple of weapons offenses. He was sentenced by Judge James Bailey to thirty months probation and nights in jail for three months.

Now it seemed that the race for Annerino's assets was on. Robert Fischer along with his attorney, Abbey Mark Botkin, claimed that Fischer was named as beneficiary of Annerino's estate. The police had found a copy of a will naming Fischer as beneficiary but it was only a copy and an original is needed in most instances to settle a probate case. Meanwhile, Annerino's two brothers and a sister filed paperwork with Judge Henry Budzinski of the Circuit Court that claimed that Annerino died without a will or intestate which would mean the estate would be split among his surviving relatives. Judge Budzinski issued an injunction that froze the bank accounts that Annerino had in seven different establishments. The judge also named Annerino's brother, August, as administrator of the estate.

In yet another bizarre twist, a lawyer named Thomas Bucaro was filing a will with the Cook County Clerk's office while the grand jury was returning the indictment on Annerino. It seemed that Annerino's most recent roommate, Roger Schumacher, 38, had retained Bucaro to conduct a search for the will. The will was stashed at the Cook County Recorder's Office. Most people don't realize that you can record any important paperwork that you have with the Recorder's office even though most individuals are only familiar with recording instruments related to the sale of real estate such as deeds. Bucaro found the will in the Recorder's office and filed it with the Cook County Clerk's office. This came as a complete surprise to Annerino's brothers and sister and Fischer insisted that they would find the will naming Fischer as the beneficiary. As it turned out, Schumacher came out on top. The will, which was signed on July 8, 1985, nullified any previous wills and named Schumacher as the sole heir to his real estate and all other property of value. He left his church to the care of Martha Kay, a long time member. He also left his sister, Clara Settino of Villa Park, $10,000 and her son $1,000.

Dwayne Coulter, Ira Jackson and Allen Falls, Jr. were found guilty by jury of the felony murder of Officer Michael Ridges as well as for the conspiracy to commit the murder of Robert Fischer. In October of 1987, Judge Bailey sentenced Coulter to natural life in prison. Falls and Jackson were given a sentence of forty years for the murder and seven years for the conspiracy to be served concurrently. Bobby Lindsey and Vincent Steven Calvin were both found guilty of conspiracy and were given four years probation with credit for twenty-seven months already served at the Cook County Jail.

As of 2004, Roger Schumacher was listed as living at Annerino's house on 28th Place. It is currently owned by a seemingly unrelated party. I attempted to make contact with the current owner but was unsuccessful. I did visit the area and I noticed a statue of the Virgin Mother in the front yard which leads me to believe that the "church" is no longer operating in the basement of the home. Falls and Jackson have since been released from prison. Coulter has continued to fight to have his conviction overturned on a number of occasions for a number of different reasons ranging from inadequate representation to prejudicial juror selection with the last ruling being as recent as 2005. All appeals have been denied. Annerino is buried with his mother and father in an unmarked grave.

Was Annerino evil from the very beginning or did his meddling with the spiritual world unleash something so horrific that it eventually ended in his own destruction and the destruction of so many others? I personally believe in a spiritual realm and there is a constant battle or struggle going on between good and evil. Many of us have heard the warnings about conducting séances or using Ouija boards to communicate with this other realm. By doing so, some believe that you extend an open invitation to the darker side of this other world whether you are aware of it or not. His "parishioners" possibly came to the church hoping to be comforted by messages from loved ones who had passed, and instead, were confronted by the darkness and negativity that Annerino brought forth. People around him ended up dead, imprisoned, or in shattered lives.

If Annerino did open this portal or gateway, did his introduction of substance abuse, government corruption, lies, greed, jealousy, hate, and wicked intentions provide a comfortable environment for evil to take root in his "church?"

The senseless end of a respectable public servant, Michael Ridges, who died when he had so much to live for and so many more to help, is, I believe, a prime indicator that some form of what we call evil was involved. Evil does exist and we don't need a séance or Ouija board to fall victim to it, so why make it easier for it to take hold.

Was it pure evil unleashed? I couldn't say with absolute certainty, but I can say that Michael Ridges died a hero doing what he loved to do. Had Ridges not been vigilant and observant that October morning almost twenty-five years ago, Coulter, Falls, and Jackson would have almost certainly succeeded in doing the bidding of an evil, vindictive, self-proclaimed minister of a sinister or otherwise misguided organization.

Grave marker of Officer Michael Ridges.

GHOST HUNTING
"CSI - The Afterlife"

I couldn't think about writing a book dealing with the paranormal from a cop's perspective without devoting a portion to that book looking at what I would consider the "Evidence Techs" or the Forensics Section of paranormal investigation.

As I had mentioned before, the first modern-day attempt at scientifically determining whether or not there was something of a conscious nature that survived death was undertaken by the American Society for Psychical Research which was founded in 1885 by Harvard psychologist and professor of philosophy, William James and other noteworthy academics of the day including Richard Hodgson, James Hyslop, Cambridge philosopher Henry Sigwick and his brilliant mathematician wife, Nora, as well as Edmund Gurney. They had taken on the task of exploring the possibility of a scientific explanation for things such as clairvoyance, ESP, communications with spirits (mediums) and other facets of a supernatural realm. By doing so they staked their reputations and careers as scientists and academics.

Ghost Hunting "CSI - The Afterlife"

There seems to be a resurgence today of individuals who are fascinated by the concept of the paranormal. You don't have to look too hard on television to find a program dealing with paranormal research

PRI, Paranormal Research of Illinois team members.

groups. They range from groups of professionals with sophisticated technological equipment to teenagers running around with video cameras set to that "creepy green nightshot setting" scaring the crap out of each other. Regardless of the type of group, they are all looking for the same thing: the elusive proof that there is something beyond the physical world that we live in.

Paranormal Research of Illinois

I recently had the opportunity to meet a local paranormal research team and observe them in action. A very good friend of mine and former gang unit partner, Eric, had let me know about a location that he was personally involved with. I had just recently let him know that I was writing a book about the paranormal and it just so happened to coincide with experiences that he and others were having at this location. I can't really divulge the actual location as of the writing of this book because the board of the corporation that oversees this particular location is not sure how it feels about the stigma of a "haunted building," however they did agree to allow a local paranormal investigation group to come in and conduct an investigation.

I can say that the location is in a northwest suburb of Chicago and that the building was built roughly sixty-five years ago by a group of firemen as a place for the firemen to socialize. The building is currently used as a hall and is rented out to groups for various functions. It consists of a large open storeroom in the front of the building which leads down a hallway to a large approximately 50' x 50' dance or dining room with a full-length, fully operational built-in wet bar. Past that is another double door leading to another smaller store room.

Eric has a hand in managing the operations of the hall and has been sitting at the bar on nights when nobody was there and has both seen and felt someone or something next to him—but only fleetingly. There has been the sound of footsteps, as if leading to the bar, and others have had heavy fire exit doors open and close by themselves and have heard things moving around in the storerooms only to find that there is nobody there. It all sounded like the sounds and sights of a "haunted" location to me. I, of course, told Eric to count me in.

The Investigation

It was a rainy, blustery Saturday night, almost stereotypical as hauntings go, and it took me about forty-five minutes to make the trip from my house to the location in question. Eric met me at the front door at about 9pm and gave me a quick tour. It was extremely well-constructed and was very nice inside. I made a comment about finding it hard to believe that a group of firemen had built this on their time off, but then again, if you know firemen like I have had the opportunity to know, you know that they all work second jobs and they all seem to have other trades that they are skilled in besides fire work.

The paranormal research group is named PRI which stands for Paranormal Research of Illinois and is headed up by its founder, Chad Griffiths. Chad and his crew were in the middle of setting up. Now we all may have our image of ghost hunters from television shows and movies, and well, *Ghostbusters*, so I didn't really know what to expect. What I did find was a great group of guys and gals who got along very well and worked together with a common purpose. Chad was a former firefighter himself so he felt pretty comfortable with the case. He started the team on September 8, 2008 with his wife, Michelle, who has acted as the case manager since its inception. The team, at the time of the writing of this book, had a core group of eight members and five that put in time where they could. PRI works on about thirty cases per year and the team donates their time and money to the venture. They do not get compensation for what they do and they use their own money to purchase equipment and supplies. I don't believe that the Federal Government yet provides grant money for ghost hunting. The backgrounds of the team members are extremely varied. Members are firemen, police officers, attorneys, stay-at-home moms; you name it. Even though they all come from very different backgrounds, their common purpose seemed to bind them all together and all seem to enjoy what they do very much. The group considers their base of operations to be Baileyville, Illinois, which is about five miles due south of Freeport, Illinois, and about fifteen to twenty miles west of Rockford, Illinois. Chad is also the founder and the administrator of the team's website.

According to Chad, the first goal of the group is to be skeptical, which I know sounds counter to what most people would think, but the team stresses that the investigation of the paranormal starts with trying to prove that it isn't. In other words they first try to determine if there is a logical, this-worldly, explanation for the phenomena that people claim to experience. In fact, their business cards state, "We believe that the only way to prove paranormal activity is to first disprove it."

I spoke to Mike Hodges, who is the technical supervisor of the group, and he also seemed like a very down-to-earth normal guy with a family that just enjoyed the thrill of exploring the unexplored and trying to explain the unexplained. As they were setting up, both Chad and Mike took the time to give me a tour of their equipment and what they use it for. Much of the equipment was similar to equipment that police departments use for traditional surveillance operations such as

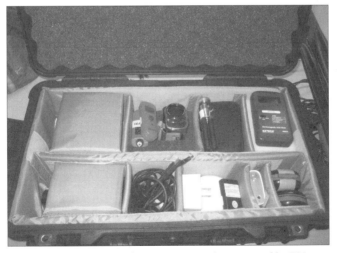

Various recording devices, thermometers, and meters used by PRI during investigations.

Chicago's Haunt Detective

One version of infrared camera used by PRI.

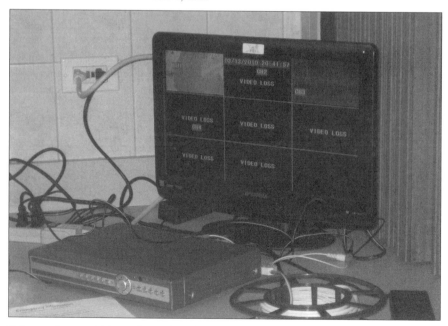

Video monitor on which we witnessed a table move in an unoccupied storage area.

video cameras and digital voice recorders, but there was some other equipment that wasn't.

I have to be honest here and admit that I have always had an issue with people using equipment to detect something that they have no physical proof of in the first place. Let's take for example something that most of us are familiar with, a smoke detector. Most of us do or should have at least one smoke detector on each floor of our houses. We know the smoke detector works because we understand the properties of fire and smoke and we can design equipment to react or detect the presence of this particular substance. I can't say that I know exactly how a smoke detector works or that I have ever designed one, but I can reasonably assume that whoever did design it, knew a little something about the properties of smoke in order to detect it. Another example, and one that probably illustrates my point a little better, is a carbon monoxide detector. I am reasonably sure, although not 100 percent, that people were dying from carbon monoxide poisoning before we knew what the substance was that was actually killing them. Carbon monoxide is invisible and odorless so our senses wouldn't be able to pick it up, but it can kill you nonetheless. Before we understood the properties of carbon monoxide, it would have been impossible to design a device that could identify or detect it reliably.

So how is it that we can try to detect a ghost or other paranormal phenomena without having a specimen of a ghost to base our detection on. It reminds me of a project that my son had in grade school in observance of St. Patrick's Day. Everyone in class had to design a leprechaun trap. It sounds silly at first, but it really did a great job teaching kids critical thinking skills. First you had to know a little bit more about a leprechaun before you could ever hope to trap one. You had to determine the different characteristics of the leprechaun such as size, weight, likes, dislikes, weaknesses and so on. We researched the leprechaun and found that they were not very large in stature so the trap didn't have to be the size of a Volkswagen. We know that they like money and other shiny materials. They are cobblers or shoemakers by profession and therefore could not pass up a shoe in need of repair or refinishing. So even though the leprechaun is a mythical creature (I know to some this is debatable; in fact I think there was an assistant state's attorney who I worked with who was a leprechaun, but I digress) the traps all had a general look and design because everyone had the same information to go on. They generally took the shape of a shoebox with a stick holding it up from the bottom with a string attached and a small dirty shoe or fake gold coins underneath. When the little guy crawled under the box to retrieve the prize, whamo! We got ourselves our very own leprechaun!

I know I have taken a long time to explain this point of view but it is just not my point of view and it is a very real point of view. Chad completely understood and I'm sure it is not the first time that he has heard that argument. In fact, he referred back to their original goal of using the equipment to root out what we would consider rational explanations for what some consider to be paranormal experiences and in the meantime, if the equipment picks up something unexplained then so be it. I can truly see his point of view and have to admit that in a way that is how scientific discovery operates. We use the technology that we currently understand to try to explain things that we don't understand yet.

I had discovered that the team had been out to this particular location one time before and planned to return again after we finished tonight for a grand total of three visits with each visit designed to concentrate on a different area of the building. The goal for this evening was to concentrate on the bar area and the rear storeroom. There were five non-team members who were made up of Eric, myself, a fire/police dispatcher, the manager of the building, and a police officer's wife who, just like the rest of us, was curious as to how this whole night was going to work out. The all-night plan (actually it turned out to be about 6am) was to have the team do their thing and for us non-team members to do what individuals at the building normally do (sit at the bar, drink, and talk) I thought I could handle that and was definitely up to the challenge.

The team started by taking baseline readings of the EMF or electromagnetic frequencies that existed in the building under normal conditions. Almost everything that is electrical in nature whether battery or AC powered give off differing amounts of EMF. It isn't that ghosts are known to put off EMF but rather a higher than normal reading in a certain area may indicate something electrical causing the "paranormal phenomena." They also usually do a scan for RF or radio frequency in the area because high levels of RF can be dangerous and has been known to cause hallucinations in individuals that also could be a rational explanation for unexplained happenings. Mike Hodges had told me of a situation where they were scanning for RF when they took readings in a bedroom of a client. The readings were in the dangerous range and they traced it to a malfunctioning clock radio in the bedroom. That may have saved the residents from some unexplained headaches in the future. Unfortunately, their RF equipment was on the blink tonight and had to be replaced so that will have to wait for their next visit.

The same logic holds true for the video cameras. The cameras may never pick up a ghost but they will definitely show if someone is attempting to fabricate the "haunting." Chad told me of a case where a couple had called the team to do an investigation of their farmhouse but in reality they were a skeptic group (remember skeptic is not a bad word!) trying to show that ghost hunting teams or paranormal research groups were a bunch of charlatans. They basically wanted to trap the team into deeming something as paranormal when the whole thing was simply an elaborate hoax. They started their investigation the same way that they always do with a sweep of the area and one of the team members discovered speaker wires running to different hidden areas in the house and they were quickly asked to leave the premises.

After the team had finished getting a baseline scan of EMF they also used digital thermometers to identify any cold or hot areas in the building that were not within the average for the building. Many people who have claimed to experience paranormal activity claim that the room would feel extremely cold shortly before or during the experience. It may not be clear at the time whether the temperature actually dropped or the individual was experiencing the cold chills or goose bumps associated with a scary or creepy experience.

Every member of the team seems to have their own area of expertise or concentration based on their skill set and personal experience and curiosity. There are audio specialists, video specialists, photographers, historians, investigators, and what they like to call HSPs or "Highly Sensitive Persons." Chad mentioned that they have two members who consider themselves to be sensitive to paranormal activity. In other words, can sense presences that can't be seen and hear things that can't be heard by someone who doesn't possess a certain degree of sensitivity. They don't go as far as to say that these members are psychic or clairvoyant, but just that they can pick up on things that the equipment may not be able to.

They also had in their arsenal, digital audio recorders with which they attempt to capture sounds that may not be immediately picked up by researchers during the investigation itself due to our natural filtering skills (car doors, trains, airplanes) or that may record EVP or "Electronic Voice Phenomena." EVP is typically picked up by a recorder and is not able to be heard until the audio is listened to after the event or after the audio is adjusted using a third party audio editor.

It is theorized that entities or spirits can use these recording devices to communicate with living persons. The digital recorder would be considered a one-way communication while the "Ghost Box" could be considered a real-time two-way communications device. The Ghost Box is actually a device that scans AM or FM radio frequencies in either a random or linear fashion creating a "white noise" that is believed to be used by spirits to respond to questions or carry on conversations with researchers. The popular belief is that Thomas Edison was working on a device like this before he died. There is however no proof that I could find that linked Thomas Edison to an interest in the paranormal or that he was working on an electric device to speak with spirits. It does make for a cool story though. Chad and his group had a device that they called the "Shack Hack" or a poor man's ghost box which was basically an AM/FM radio that was converted to randomly scan frequencies.

The investigation was underway and the EMF and temperature sweeps had been conducted. I tended bar (very poorly by the way) and we carried on various conversations that one would have when one expected to be taking part in a paranormal investigation for the next eight hours. The only time we had to be silent was when they were taking EVP samples near where we were sitting. Jim Prewitt, who was the trainer and HSP of the group, was picking up a sense that there was a presence near the bar area. He was scribbling notes on a pad of paper and right after Eric had said something about Vodka, Jim turned his pad around and showed that he had written exactly what Eric had just said. He wouldn't have had time to scribble it down after he said it and it didn't seem to coincide with any other conversation at the time, so it was not as if he could have naturally predicted what Eric was going to say based on the conversation. I have to admit that it was a little freaky, but then again that was what we all were kind of hoping for in the first place. It doesn't necessarily support the theory that Jim was picking up spirits, although sometimes Eric may seem dead. (I love you man!) but it did more or less show that he had something going on.

As the night progressed, the team was busy doing their thing and they readjusted cameras and redirected investigations and teams within their team. I was beginning to think that Jim's prediction of Eric's vodka statement was going to be the extent of it when we heard a loud scraping or shuffling coming from the back store room. I happened to be across from the monitor that was displaying the infrared camera in the storeroom at the time that the noise was going on and had to rub my eyes because I was legitimately watching a table sliding across the floor! We ran into the room which of course was empty and I looked at the table that I had seen on the monitor. It wasn't moving while we were in the room, but I had seen it before when Eric had shown me the room on our initial tour of the building. I couldn't say for sure that I remembered exactly the way the table was sitting when I had seen it the first time, but I do know that the table was old, round, and very heavy. I didn't see anyone else in the room at the time on the screen and it wasn't as though I had tabs on everyone in the team to rule out a hoax, but I do know what I saw and it would have been very difficult for anyone to have left the room and gotten by us since we were literally twenty-five feet from the entrance and would have heard someone running through the back door. I did think that they could have videotaped a segment of the storeroom on the last visit and rigged it to play back while we were watching as though it were real time but it didn't explain how they could have synched the noise in the back room with the action on the camera!

The rest of the evening went along without any incident and we shut down at about 5:30am. The building had a Girl Scouting Function starting at about 7:30am.

Overall it was a very fun and enlightening experience. It was obvious that the team loved what they were doing and had a special bond. They took the investigation very seriously and worked well together for a team that has not been working together for a long time even though individual members have varying degrees of experience with other teams.

I really wanted to thank Chad and his team for allowing me to take part. I would encourage you to check out their website at http://www. paranormal-research-of-illinois.com. It contains bios on the members, inventories of the type of equipment they use, cases that clients have allowed them to post publicly as well as a glossary and blog.

PSYCHIC DETECTIVES

The idea of psychics lending their skills to help solve criminal cases has been around since there have been criminal investigations and psychics. I will admit that there have been a number of cases that I have been involved with where I wish I was psychic. Actually there have been some supervisors that I have worked for who expected me to be psychic but that's another story for another therapy session.

I can say from personal experience that I have worked with absolutely no psychics on any criminal cases in my own little law enforcement world. I do however read on occasion that a police department is working with a psychic in order to solve a missing persons case or a cold murder case. I can say that our department did not have any guidelines or standard operating procedures for working with psychics and the other departments that I had contacted did not either. My search however was not exhaustive. My educated guess is that a vast majority of departments do not have standard operating procedures for dealing with psychics. I don't think that it is because they have an axe to grind with psychics. I think it is just that they would have to treat a "psychic" just as they would any witness.

My feeling and the feeling of many officers that I have spoken with is that they would listen to anyone who thought they had information that would help them in a case. We owe it to a family, especially in a missing person case and/or murder case, to look under every stone.

One of the first problems that I can see with being a psychic supplying information is that the psychic themselves may find themselves in an uncomfortable position, especially if their information is "right on the money." Imagine you are the investigating officer in a case where there is a missing child and an individual comes to the police station because they want to let you know that the young child is dead. The person goes on to explain how they were killed, when they were killed, and where you can find the body! I don't know about you, but that sounds remarkably similar to a confession. Things can get real sticky if what this person says checks out to be accurate. You can quickly see how this particular psychic may be late for their next scheduled appointment. The truth is that rarely does anything like that happen. I am not saying that there haven't been psychics who have supplied information on cases that ultimately was found to be credible. It just isn't the case that they supply all of the details in such specifics, all of the time.

I was very curious about the extent to which law enforcement utilizes psychic information, how they use it and how the relationship with the psychic is developed.

It is more common for the family of a victim or missing person to contact a psychic (or "sensitive" as some like to be referred to as), than it is for the police department to initiate the call, although it does happen. A family member or friend may reach out for help for any number of reasons. Some may be unhappy with the progress of an investigation or may not fell as though their case has been given ample attention. Some may feel that they need to help and cannot just sit back and "do nothing." Others may have had positive experiences with psychics who have helped them or others in the past.

In still other instances it is the psychic or sensitive who contacts a police department themselves because of a feeling, vision, or dream that has enabled them to see or feel critical information that they legitimately wish to share in order to help a particular case.

Unfortunately, there are also those unscrupulous few who are merely looking to get their name in print. Typically, they will call many different departments with information about a crime, and by playing a numbers game, may happen upon a case that seems to fit the information that they are providing. They are of course betting that the departments that do not have cases that fit will simply not report the call. But the one out of a hundred that does fit will somehow make the newspaper. Let's face it, a newspaper article about a psychic helping to solve a crime is more interesting than a psychic who gets it all wrong.

Ernesto Montgomery

I came across an amusing article in a June 13, 1979 edition of the *Chicago Tribune* to illustrate the prior information. The article was written by Marilynn Preston and concerns a prediction of the infamous crash of American Airlines flight 191 which crashed on take-off from O'Hare International Airport in Chicago enroute to Los Angeles on May 25, 1979. All 271 persons including the crew were killed along with 2 people on the ground.

Preston had received a press release from a man named Ernesto Montgomery who claimed to be a psychic with a 99 to 99½ percent accuracy rate and a tremendous background. He also claimed that he had been a police officer for over twenty years, a member of the British Intelligence Psychic Division, an acclaimed Jamaican International Psychic, spiritual adviser, religious consultant, head of the Universal Metaphysical Church, Inc., and Ernesto Montgomery Crusades. In the press release, Montgomery claims to have sent the President of American Airlines in Los Angeles a letter dated May 10, 1978, in which he states that Flight 161 from Chicago to Los Angeles would crash on May 25, 1978. He also stated that he attempted to have *The Dallas Morning News* print the prediction in their classified ads in order to prove his prediction was credible but was denied the ability to do so in writing because the ad did not conform to the paper's guidelines for ads. Even though the "6" in his prediction should have been "9," if Montgomery checked out, it would be quite an incredible prediction.

Preston first called American Airlines and spoke with a vice president who told her that if she sent the letter at all it should have gone to New York and not Los Angeles. He stated that American Airlines has no record of the letter and does not have time to deal with all the kooks, cranks, and crazies that crawl out of the floorboards every time there is a disaster. Preston then attempted to contact *The Dallas Morning News* and they produced the ad that Montgomery was referring to, but it had nothing to do with a prediction. It was an ad for a home study course in metaphysics! Preston then contacted the Los Angeles Police Department since it actually conducted a study of psychics as they may relate to police investigation. (I will be referencing the results of that study later in the book.) Preston spoke with a psychologist, Louise Ludwig, who stated that she is responsible for selecting the psychics used in their study and recalled Montgomery. She said that she read his literature and he seemed to be too hungry for publicity and he was not chosen for the research study. Preston then contacted a man by the name of Robert Nelson who ran what was called the Central Premonitions Registry out of New York. This was a clearing house where psychics could register their predictions so that they would be on file before the predicted event occurred. Nelson said that he was unable to help because he hadn't opened the mail in months! Preston felt confident that she had checked Montgomery out and called him directly with her findings.

Montgomery dismissed American Airlines because he didn't think that they would admit to knowing about a disaster that they could have averted. He also had never heard about the Premonition Registry in New York. When she mentioned the fact about the classified ad information not checking out, things got weird. Montgomery stated,

> *"I have been in this field since I was 5 years old. I was born with two appendages below both ears. They are like little bones, maybe 1/16 of an inch or so, but when I am about to pick up psychic vibrations about the future, they shoot out to a length of 2 or 3 inches! Think of your TV antenna!"*

Preston ended the article at that point. In police work we would consider the antenna statement made by Montgomery as what we would call a "clue."

Unfortunately, persons such as Montgomery are a big factor in why police departments would rather not talk about using or consulting with psychics in criminal or missing persons cases. There is also the factor of ridicule and "cranking" that they would be subject to by other departments and even within the department. The fact is that people are under the impression from television shows and newspaper articles that police departments routinely using psychics to help solve cases or may even have a "Psychic Division" similar to let's say a Homicide or Burglary Division. Nothing could be further from the truth.

Police departments are ultimately made up of people just like you and me, even though it may not seem that way initially. While the judicial system as a whole may not officially recognize the significance of or even the existence of psychic phenomenon, individuals within the system may. I mentioned earlier in the book about my own personal experiences that have shaped my attitude toward the subject. My attitude is the same as many investigators. I would never turn away any witness who believes that they have information that could possibly help an investigation, especially with one involving missing persons or potential homicide investigations.

Los Angeles P.D. Psychic Evaluations

An Evaluation of the Use of Psychics in the Investigation of Major Crimes

From 1978 to 1980, The Los Angeles Police Department's Behavioral Science Section conducted an evaluation of psychics to determine whether there might be any merit to utilizing psychics as an investigative tool. Martin Reiser was the director of the section and was assisted by clinical researchers at UCLA and Los Angeles City College. They conducted two separate studies. The first study concluded in 1979 and was entitled, "An Evaluation of the Use of Psychics in the Investigation of Major Crimes" which was published in March of 1979 in the Journal of Police Science and Administration. The study involved using 12 psychics selected by the researchers and involved sealed envelopes containing information and material related to two solved crimes and two unsolved crimes.

Reiser was actually optimistic about the results and said that if they determined that psychic information was useful in solving crimes that the department would definitely use them as a tool. At the conclusion of the first study, however, Reiser expressed his disappointment by concluding, "Overall, little, if any, information was elicited from the 12 psychic participants that would provide material helpful in the investigation of the major crimes in question."

It is interesting to note that in the purpose statement of the study on page 18 of the aforementioned journal, Reiser states, "The purpose was not to address the question of the existence of ESP or paranormal phenomena generally, but only to confront the narrower issue of the usefulness of this kind of information in the solution of major crimes at this police agency [LAPD] at this time."

The study ran into most of the problems that are associated with psychic impressions and one of those problems is that you can't simply read off of a list of questions for the psychic to answer. In order to quantify the results and standardize the answers, the researchers listed different categories of crime details for all of the four test cases. In crime No. 1 there were 21 categories, Crime No. 2 had 33 categories, Crime No. 3 had 29 categories, and Crime No. 4 had 29 categories. These categories ranged from as detailed as victim's and suspect's name to as general as the type of crime or sex of victim or suspect. It is also noteworthy to add that the researchers used 8 of what they considered professional psychics who derive income from their position and 4 amateur psychics who claimed to have gifts but did not charge for their services.

The psychics were asked to hold sealed envelopes with material and some evidence from the actual crimes and asked for their impressions. They were then allowed to open the envelopes and handle the physical items to see if handling the items would elicit a different response. The term used to describe the psychic's use of physical objects to derive impressions is referred to as psychometry.

One issue that was difficult to overcome was the fact that a psychic's impressions couldn't be restricted to just the form. They more or less had to let the psychic present the impression and they would derive the parts of the impression that matched the details of the crimes in the study. For instance, one psychic's response was, "I get a man, black. I hear screaming, screaming. I'm running up stairs and down. My head...

someone bounces my head on the wall or floor. I see trees—a park? In the city, but green. Did this person live there? What does the number '2' mean? I get a bad, bloody taste in my mouth. The names 'John' or 'Joseph' or something like that. I am running on the street like crazy. This is a very serious crime. I can't hold the envelope in my hand."

This response was one of the briefer responses but you can see how it would be difficult to resist interpreting the meaning of the impression and to pull out only the pertinent details (black man, park, city, stairs, physical trauma, the color green, the number 2, and so on).

Interestingly, the psychic labeled as psychic 6A (an amateur psychic) in crime 4 managed to get the most hits on a single case which amounted to a 6 out of 29 correct. The psychic hit on the sex and height of the victim, the cause of death, the crime, and the sex and eye color of the suspect. Overall, however, the results were not all that impressive. The average score was a 2.7 which the researchers attributed to no better than chance.

The second study entitled, "A Comparison of Psychics, Detectives, and Students in the Investigation of Major Crimes," was concluded in 1980. Once again the study was a double-blind and included 12 psychics, 11 college students, and 12 homicide detectives. They again used four cases, two solved and two unsolved, which were chosen by an individual not involved in the study. The psychic group created 10 times more information than the other groups but, according to Rieser, did not produce any better information than the other two groups. Although there was the occasional surprise, such as when a psychic felt that a church was involved in one of the cases and the case did involve the murder of a church official, the psychics did not fare any better than chance.

I have to admit that 12 is not a very large number and it could be that the department simply chose the "wrong" 12 psychics to test, but whatever the case, it didn't look good for the psychics.

Psychics: Do Police Departments Really Use Them?

An article by Jane Ayers Sweat and Mark W. Drum appeared in the Winter 1993 edition of the *Skeptical Inquirer* entitled, "Psychics: Do Police Departments Really Use Them?" The *Skeptical Inquirer* is published by the Committee for Skeptical Inquiry which was started in

1976 to scientifically and objectively examine claims of extraordinary or "paranormal" claims.

The authors sent a 5-question survey to the 50 largest police departments in the United States. The first question on the survey was, "In the past has your Police Department used psychics or does the department presently use them in solving investigations?" The result from the 48 departments who answered the survey was that 31 departments had not and 17 had. I actually thought that the number of departments who had was surprisingly high, roughly 35 percent. The authors seemed to indicate that they thought the number was actually low. (I would have predicted around less than 10 percent, so I guess my psychic skills are lacking.)

The second question broke down the types of cases that psychics were used for. Of the 17 departments who answered *yes* to the first questions, 15 used them for homicides, 10 for missing persons, 1 for kidnapping, 1 for sexual assault and 1 for burglary.

The third question had to do with whether psychic information was handled any differently as an ordinary source. The vast majority of those who answered the question (33 out of 40 respondents) responded that they didn't treat it any differently. Seven answered *yes*.

Question 4 asked if the information the department received was any more helpful in solving a case than other information received and the unanimous answer (26 respondents) was *no*.

The fifth question asked the departments if psychic information was "more valuable." Ninety-five percent of the 41 departments who answered this question indicated that psychic information was "no more valuable than any other information," however, there was one department that answered "sometimes" and one department that stated that it "depended on the psychic used."

Again, I was surprised to find that so many large departments had used psychics before, but the fact that none of the departments responded that psychic information was helpful is a strike against the usefulness of psychic information to a criminal investigation. We should keep in mind that neither of the studies intended to prove or disprove paranormal abilities or ESP but addressed the usefulness of such information by law enforcement. One must also keep in mind that the use of a psychic or the usefulness of a psychic may be something that a department does not wish to share in a public document much in the same way that a department may not want to divulge their investigative process at all so as to not give future perpetrators any foreknowledge or advantage.

Jack The Ripper Apprehended?

Aside from the occasional Ernesto Montgomery and the resistance of psychic impressions to conform to the needs of law enforcement, there is also the matter of the intentional hoax that can hinder the legitimacy of psychic information as well as the misled, but well-intentioned, author who perpetuates such hoaxes.

In doing the research for this book, I had come across a story in a book entitled, *Crime and the Psychic World*, by Fred Archer and published by William Morrow and Company, Inc., New York, 1969.

The first case on page 15 of the book was entitled, "Human Bloodhound Tracked Jack The Ripper."

The story centers around Robert James Lees. Lees was more of a spiritual man of the biblical sense, a scholar and a philanthropist, but according to Archer performed séances for Queen Victoria. Archer claims that the story came about after a document was discovered following the death of Lees. Archer also claims to have been acquainted with Lees'

LONDON'S HORROR AGAIN.

ANOTHER CHAPTER IN THE STORY OF THE WHITECHAPEL MURDERS.

The President of the Vigilance Committee Receives by Parcel Post Half of the Kidney of One of the Slain Women, with a Letter from the Mysterious Assassin Saying He Had Eaten the Other Half—Other News and Gossip by Cable.

The murderer known as Jack the Ripper terrorized the residents of the Whitechapel District of London in 1888.

son, Claude Lees and to have known his daughter, Miss Eva Lees "for many years."

The story begins in the autumn of 1888. Lees was working in his study when he became overwhelmed by a psychic vision. In the vision he could see a man and a woman walking down a London street at night illuminated by the light of a local gin palace. He could see a clock through a pub's window and it appeared that the clock read 12:40. The woman appeared drunk and the man was wearing a suit of dark tweed and carried a light overcoat.

The two ducked into a narrow court and the woman leaned back against a wall. The man approached her but with a menacing look. He glanced around quickly, cupped his hand over the woman's mother and then quickly and quietly slit her throat.

Robert James Lees, 1895.

Blood spurted over the man's white shirt and he held onto the woman as she slid against the wall and onto the ground. He then began to mutilate her body and when finished he cleaned the knife on her clothing and covered his shirt with the overcoat. He then strolled away at a normal pace as to not attract attention.

When Lees awoke from the shock of the vision he hurried to Scotland Yard where he was treated as just another kook coming out of the woodwork following the start of the Ripper crimes. The police official did however write down the time and description of the crime. The crime happened the following night.

Lees had returned to the scene of the crime and could not bear being in the location. He took his family on a short vacation abroad in order to ease he nerves.

On returning to London, he and his wife were aboard an omnibus that stopped at Notting Hill. A man in a dark tweed suit and light overcoat boarded. He knew instantly that he was in the presence of a murderer. He whispered to his wife that the man was Jack The Ripper! When the man exited at Marble Arch, Lees followed him. The man turned down Park Lane and Lees followed closely. As luck would have it, Lees spotted a police officer and immediately pointed out the man and stated that he was Jack The Ripper and demanded that the man be taken into custody. The officer thought again that Lees was crazy and threatened to arrest him. As they were arguing, the man boarded a cab and was driven out of sight.

That same night, Lees had a similar vision. It wasn't as vivid as the previous vision but he could see the victim's face clearly. One ear had been severed and the other was barely hanging from the head.

Lees again went to Scotland Yard and again he was treated like a lunatic until he mentioned the part about the ears. At the mention of the ears, the officer's demeanor changed. According to the story, Scotland Yard had just received a letter from the *Central News Agency* from an individual claiming to be Jack The Ripper. In the letter he threatens to cut off the ears of the victim and send them to the police.

The next night there were more than four thousand police, many disguised as dock workers or seamen, scouring the streets of the Whitechapel neighborhood. Supposedly, even with this amount of police presence, the Ripper was able to kill two more victims that night, although in one case, he was interrupted before he could complete the severing of the victim's ears.

Lees supposedly suffered another nervous breakdown as a result of the news, and after his recovery, attended a dinner with American friends, Roland B. Shaw of New York and Fred C. Beckwith of Wisconsin. During dinner, Lees exclaimed, "Jack the Ripper has committed another murder!"

This time Scotland Yard took him seriously. They took Lees to the scene of the crime and shortly thereafter, like a human bloodhound, had a "scent." Lees guided the police from the East End to the West End. He stopped in front of an impressive mansion out of breath and eyes bloodshot. He stated to the police that the murderer was inside. The chief inspector could not believe it. The house was owned by a highly respected and wealthy physician!

The inspector asked Lees to tell him what was on the other side of the door and if Lees was correct than the investigation could continue.

Lees stated that there was a black oak porter's chair in the hallway to the right, a stained glass window at one end and a large mastiff sleeping at the foot of the stairs.

The police knocked on the door and the maid opened the door. They could see the chair and the stained glass window but no dog. They questioned the maid and she stated that there was a mastiff sleeping by the stairs but that she had just let it out into the garden.

They spoke to the doctor's wife who confided in them that soon after they were married, she became aware her husband's troubling obsession with wanting to inflict pain. She walked into the kitchen one time to find her husband torturing the family cat. She left before her husband realized that she was in the room. The next morning her husband was as normal and friendly as usual. His manias became more frequent and more violent. At one point, he was beating his small son in order to punish him for imitating his father's cruelty and became so violent that the servants had to help in order to restrain him.

His wife became extremely troubled when she realized that her husband would be absent from home on the same nights as the Ripper murders.

When the doctor himself came downstairs, it didn't take long for him to admit that he suffered from episodes of lost memory. He remembered on occasion waking up from a stupor in his study and one time he woke with blood on his shirt! When faced with the possibility that he was Jack the Ripper, he begged the police to kill him.

The doctor was apprehended, but was not killed. A specially formed commission on lunacy was formed and a secret hearing was held. The commission committed the man to a lunatic asylum. The story and name of the Ripper were never released and Lees was sworn to secrecy which was an oath he never violated.

According to Fred Archer, the story was based upon a document that was not to be opened until Lees' death.

In actuality, the story is based upon an article published in the *Chicago Times Herald* on April 28, 1895, and republished in the British tabloid, *The Sunday People*, on May 19.1895. I retrieved a copy of the 1895 *Chicago Times Herald* article and it is fairly easy to see where Archer got his material from. The article is supposedly a retelling of the story by a London doctor by the name of Dr. Howard who supposedly served on the lunacy commission that committed the physician accused of the Ripper murders. This Dr. Howard supposedly told a man by the name of William Greer Harrison of the Bohemia Club of San Francisco the story during a bit of vulnerability due to excess consumption of wine.

There are whole sections of Archer's account that look as if they were copied verbatim from the Chicago article. If there did exist a document that was sealed until Lee's death, then Lees also must have copied it from the article. I find it highly unlikely that Lees and a doctor who supposedly served on the lunacy commission would have related the story almost verbatim at two separate times and in two separate documents. Author, Melvin Harris, in his book, *Jack the Ripper, The Bloody Truth* theorized that the Chicago article was a hoax perpetrated by members of the Chicago "Whitechapel Club," which had its offices behind *The Chicago Times Herald's* offices. The Whitechapel Club was a press club for budding journalists known for its morbid décor which included lamp shades and drinking cups made from human skulls.

Whether Fred Archer knowingly took the story from the papers of 1895 and committed a fraud, or whether he indeed had heard a rumor of a document supposedly opened after Lees' death and attributed the information from the article as being similar to the article, I do not know. The original article could not be authenticated and had numerous historical inaccuracies. Lees did go to Scotland Yard to profess his visions but not during the month of any Ripper killings and there were only five killings attributed to Jack the Ripper and not seventeen killings as referenced in the article and Archer's rendition.

Either way, if someone does not conduct the proper background research of a supposed psychic event, you could find yourself as the unwitting pawn in an elaborate hoax.

Mel Doerr
Professional Psychic

I wanted to begin with a psychic or "sensitive," as some like to be referred to, who has been contacted by authorities in the past (and not the reverse). In this way, I could look at the subject objectively and at someone who had worked with police departments in the past. (Remember that I have had my own experiences with precognition.) I also wanted to choose someone who didn't seem like a media hog. I ended up calling the offices of Mel Doerr in Mount Prospect. One of the main reasons that I had chosen Mel was the fact that one of the most recent cases I had found involved the Lake County Coroner's Office who had contacted Mr. Doerr on a cold case involving an unidentified skull.

I initially contacted Mr. Doerr via email and explained that I was writing a book and he was more than happy to sit down and speak with me. I contacted his receptionist, Barbara, who was very pleasant on the phone, and set up an initial meeting. I had never visited a psychic before and really didn't know what to expect. When I arrived at his office in Mt. Prospect, I was surprised that there was simply white lettering on a glass door that read, "Offices of Mel Doerr." I guess maybe I expected large colorful signs with pictures of hands with eyeballs in the palms and other colorful wooden signs that said "Psychic Readings." Upon entering I noticed that the office was being rearranged for a seminar that they were having in a few weeks but overall the décor was a mixture of Egyptian, Native American, and Hawaiian motifs.

I met Barbara who was just as pleasant in person as she was on the phone. She also mentioned that she was the hypnotherapist in the office. She informed me that Mel was currently with a client and I had an opportunity to meet a long-time client of Mel's while I was waiting.

Her name was Josephine, and while she looked to be in her 60s she was proud to mention that she was recently celebrating her 89th birthday! She was so full of energy and really had less gray hair than I do and I am 43. (She swears that she didn't treat her hair although she had recently had it styled and wanted to let Mel take a look at it.) She mentioned that she had known Mel for the past twenty-five years and just loved him. We started chatting and somehow I mentioned that I had grown up in Cicero. She had a memory like a steel trap and started talking about meeting Al Capone's brother Ralph. (You can't mention the name Cicero without somehow finding your way into a conversation about the Capone family.) She went on to say that when she was 18, she was very gullible and had gone to a local tavern with some of her friends to interview for a job with Ralph, the owner of the bar. She didn't realize that she was interviewing for the position of "call girl." She mentioned how different Ralph was from Al. She said that Ralph was thinner, taller, and better looking than his brother. She also mentioned that she thankfully didn't get the job.

I told her it was probably because she was so gullible and innocent and he probably thought that she would present a problem later on. She simply said, "Naw, I just think I wasn't good looking enough."

We eventually got onto the subject of the finer points of eating tripe when Mel exited his office.

Mel was very personable and friendly and invited me into his office. I could get a sense from the way he talked to Josephine and me that he had a genuine interest in people and his clients seemed to have a genuine interest in him. Mel seemed very open and not as evasive or defensive as I expected him to be. I asked him how he found himself in the business of being a professional psychic and he mentioned that he came from a family that had psychic ability. He told me that his father had psychic ability and that ability seemed to have passed to him. His earliest recollection of his ability was when his mother had picked him up from school when he was six years old. When he got into the car, he remembers telling his mom that his grandfather had just died and sure enough he did die unexpectedly that day.

Mel was born and raised in Louisville, Kentucky, and decided to go into psychology because he thought that would give him the best opportunity to try to explain this gift that he had been given. He moved to Chicago after college and spent ten years in the field of psychology before he decided to pursue his career as a psychic. I mentioned that I had had some experience with a precognitive event and mentioned the dream that I had as a child, but I also made it clear that I considered myself a skeptical believer. He was well aware of all the arguments against the existence of psychic abilities and was used to working with and welcomed skeptical inquiry. He also knew about my former profession from our previous emails and I reminded him about our creed, "In God We Trust, all others need I.D."

There were a couple of things that Mel wanted to make clear during our discussion. One was the fact that he believes that psychics do not solve crimes. They merely provide another source of information for law enforcement to use in order for them to solve crimes or find missing persons. The other fact is that he never charges a fee for any work he does for a law enforcement agency. One of the main arguments against using psychics in criminal investigations is the waste of taxpayers' money.

Since I had never worked with a psychic in my law enforcement career, I was curious as to how and when a psychic is consulted. Mel is normally contacted by family members of victims or missing persons. I was curious about the Lake County skull case that originally attracted my attention to Mel in the first place.

Psychic Detectives

Mel Doerr in his Mt. Prospect office. *Courtesy of Mel Doerr.*

Case#1:

The Lake County Skull

Mel Doerr was contacted by Lake County Coroner, Dr. Richard Keller, in March of 2008, during a routine review of Lake County cold cases.

In 1991, about three days after Christmas, an off-duty military police officer was walking near the cemetery at Ft. Sheridan when he noticed a skull (just the facial area and one tooth remained) mounted on a fallen tree with a branch poking through an eye socket. The Lake Forest police were notified and the skull was recovered along with an orange raincoat and sleeves of an undershirt. Later in the day, an officer by the name of Matthew Deidrich recovered a 27-inch metal sword and burlap from inside of a hollowed-out tree about 50 yards from where the skull was found. Mel told me that the police had thought maybe the skull was related to some satanic or black magic rituals, but Mel said that he did not get that impression.

A check of the National Crime Information Center databases turned up no dental record or missing persons case matches. In the early 1990s, the skull was sent to different anthropological and forensics groups to try to identify the remains. The University of Illinois at Chicago believed it was the skull of an African-American or American Indian woman 25-60 years old. An anthropologist at Judson College believed it was an American Indian woman between 18 and 50 years of age. A group of forensic dentists concluded that the skull was that of a woman about 40 to 60 years old. The skull remained in the coroner's office for the next 16 years.

Doerr said that he many times uses psychometry, or the interpretation of impressions or feelings derived from the touching of physical objects, when working on cases. He had handled the skull on a number of occasions over the course of about five weeks. He eventually determined that the woman was about 40 years old and of African-American descent. He stated that he felt very dizzy at times while holding the skull and that indicated that the woman had committed suicide and he believes it involved a rope and therefore the woman probably had hanged herself. He felt that the woman was in an abusive domestic situation that she felt there was no escape from. He also experienced a strange taste in his mouth that he attributed to the presence of a drug or alcohol addiction issue. He believes that her remains had washed down a ravine and came to rest near the spot where the skull was found.

I asked Doerr how Dr. Keller knew of him, and he said that he has worked with police departments in the past and that Dr. Keller had taken some classes at the Infinity Foundation in Highland Park, Illinois, where Doerr is a faculty member.

The remains have since been sent to the Center for Human Identification in Texas which is funded by the National Institute for Justice. A Dr. Harrell Gill-King is scheduled to perform chemical tests on the skull in an attempt to better identify the age of the skull as well as possible DNA tests.

Doerr feels that the saddest part about this case is that these remains belong to a human being who walked this Earth and nobody knows who she is.

As he was telling me this story you could see that he was emotionally affected during the retelling. I asked him if any other cases that he has worked on had affected him emotionally and he related to me the story of Sandra Allard.

Case#2:

Sandra Allard

Du Page County, Illinois

While Doerr was working on a local cable show called *Lifestyles* he was approached by the daughter of Sandra Allard who was working as an intern on the show.

She had requested Doerr's assistance in helping with an investigation surrounding the murder of her mother. Doerr, along with Linda Petrine, another psychic that Doerr has worked with in the past, Ms. Allard's daughter, and two deputies with the Du Page County Sheriff's Office proceeded to do a "walk-thru" of Allard's townhouse located on Theresa Court in the Gingerbrook subdivision of unincorporated York Township in Du Page County, Illinois.

The home had recently been rehabbed since the murder, so there was no physical evidence of the crime still visible. As they entered the kitchen, Doerr looked up at the ceiling and told the deputies that there was something not right with the ceiling. He felt very troubled by the ceiling. They approached the stairway leading to the second floor where Petrine had mentioned she felt that an injury had occurred. (Doerr actually was specific with me regarding the injury that Petrine had mentioned which he said was confirmed with the deputies but one that had not been released to the public.) As they entered the bedroom, Doerr fell into a trance and found himself feeling injuries to a specific area of his body that he related to the deputies. This again was confirmed as an injury that Allard had sustained but had not been released to the public. (Again, Doerr was forthright with me on details but because this is still an unsolved open case, I cannot, out of respect for the law enforcement community and the family, release any of these details which might jeopardize the investigation.)

It was public information that Allard had been stabbed numerous times and that her townhouse had been set ablaze. It was Petrine who stated to the deputies how the fire was started and how it was specifically set. This fact again was shared with me and according to Doerr, confirmed by the deputies. I can honestly say that I had never heard of a fire starting that way and cannot believe that it was just a lucky guess on Petrine's part. While in the bedroom, Doerr mentioned another strange occurrence that made the hairs on my neck stand up. While everyone was in the bedroom, a rattling noise was coming from inside the closet. Doer said that it was loud enough to make the deputies believe that someone was in the closet and they went as far as to draw their weapons. However, they soon discovered that the closet was empty.

Since it is public information that there was a fire involved in the murder, I can mention information that was relayed to Doerr by the deputies concerning the fire. If you recall, Doerr had felt troubled by the ceiling in the kitchen. The deputies had shared with Doerr that the flames that burned Allard's body were so hot that they burned through the bedroom floor and that Allard's legs were dangling through the ceiling of the kitchen on the first floor exactly in the spot that Doerr pointed to!

While all of this sounds rather uncanny, Doerr told me that sometimes a psychic cannot be completely sure about where they are receiving their impressions or visions and he believes that many times he or other psychics may be picking up impressions from others in the room such as from investigators. The investigators had obviously been on the scene soon after the murder and were privy to all of the details of the case so it would be conceivable that

Elmhurst Memorial Hospital where Sandra Allard worked as a nurse.

they were picking up the thoughts of the investigators rather than impressions from the victims or the suspects.

In spite of that fact, Doerr is of the opinion that the crime was committed by more than one person and that it was a murder-for-hire scenario. He was given information that Allard was a student

of astrology and that she gave private consultations in her home. She was also a nurse at Elmhurst Hospital and, according to newspaper accounts, conducted drug counseling sessions from home as well. He believes that someone close, possibly even a family member had hired individuals to pose as potential clients thereby gaining entry to the townhome with no evidence of force. He also seems to think that whoever committed the crime may have tried to make it look like a ritual killing because they may not have understood the difference between astrology, black magic, or satanic worship.

Allard had divorced her husband in 1988 and lived alone in the house. Her former husband denied any involvement in the murder of his ex-wife and was cooperative with investigators. Doerr stated that he does not believe that the ex-husband was involved.

It is unclear whether any information that Petrine or Doerr provided to authorities will be of help in solving the crime. The case remains unsolved.

Chicago's Haunt Detective

Case # 3:

Dr. Xu "Sue" Wang

Darien, Illinois

Yijun Zeng and Xu Wang met in China when they were medical students and had been married since 1983. They moved to the United States in 1990 and worked at the University of Chicago Hospitals. Zeng had developed Parkinson's disease and was forced to stop doing diabetes research in 1996. They moved briefly to Tulsa, Oklahoma, but ultimately came back to the Chicago area where Dr. Wang secured a position with Rush-Copley Medical Center in Aurora, Illinois. According to the *Chicago Tribune* of August 28, 2000, Zeng had reported his wife missing on August 11, 1999 when co-workers had reported that she never arrived at work. Her red Toyota was discovered shortly after her disappearance on a gravel parking area at the Waterfall Glen Forest Preserve. A few days later her pager was found off of a nearby frontage road at the intersection of Cass Avenue and Interstate Highway 55 (Stevenson Expressway) with messages still on it. The police were unable to find any other trace of the missing physician.

As the case started to cool, one of the detectives working the case, Greg Cheaure, remembered seeing an episode of "Unsolved Mysteries" in which an Arkansas psychic by the name of Carol Pate had helped Benton, Arkansas, authorities find a missing nursing home resident.

I had an opportunity to speak with the now Sgt. Greg Cheaure who is still with the Darien Police Department. Sgt. Cheaure confirmed that he contacted Pate after he had spoken with a Lieutenant from the department featured on the television show. He said that the Lieutenant from Arkansas thought what Pate had done was uncanny. He said that they had been searching for the person for some time and had used helicopters, dogs, police on horseback and over 100 volunteers over the course of two days with no luck. He said that when Pate showed up, she held the resident's eyeglasses and said that she could see the person alive and sitting next to a wall. She started walking in a certain direction and the officers had tried to stop her and told her that witnesses had believed that the resident had gone off in the opposite direction. Pate was insistent in continuing in the direction that she was going and after about an hour they came to a wall next to a freeway culvert. Pate asked what was on the other side of the wall and the Lieutenant said his hair stood up on end. They checked behind the wall and there was the resident sitting on a rock and in good condition.

Cheaure spoke with his Chief of Police, Ron Campo, and they decided to send Pate pictures of the victim and the victim's husband. They conducted a conference call with Pate and she said that she was of the opinion that Wang was dead. She said that she felt death. She believed that Wang had been strangled by her husband. Investigators had a feeling that Zeng was not being completely cooperative prior to speaking with Pate. She also mentioned something about the clothes that she would be wearing when found. Cheaure couldn't divulge the details of the clothing or other details of Pate's impressions because the case is still open. He did say that she described a building in the conversation and everyone recognized it as an extended-stay hotel in Darien. She also mentioned that the red Toyota was purposely left at the location where they found it as a diversion.

Cheaure stated that they had planned on bringing Pate to Darien from Arkansas, but a private investigator he knew was working on a case in Chicago involving the disappearance of sisters, Tionda and Diamond Bradley. Carol Pate was consulting on that case and was going to be in the area anyway. They conducted a search of the area that Pate described using cadaver dogs and came up empty except for some bones that were discarded from someone's meal that the dogs had "hit" on. Cheaure said that Pate did not provide any further details and there has been no further communication with her. They have had no further breaks in the case and it remains unsolved to this day.

The wooded area surrounding Argonne National Laboratory where a search for Dr. Wang's body was unsuccessfully conducted.

City of Darien Police Department, Darien, Illinois.

Case #4:

Eyvonne Bender and Susan Ovington

Morton Grove, Illinois

I decided to include the following case because it seems that the authorities not only utilized psychics in this case, but also hypnosis. Eyvonne Bender was from Skokie, while Susan Ovington was from Morton Grove. Both girls were 17 years old and their bodies were discovered at 9:30pm just off the bicycle path in the St. Paul Woods Forest Preserve. Both girls were partially nude and had been shot to death. A pool of blood had been discovered about fifty feet away with bloody drag marks leading to where the bodies were discovered hidden behind bushes and shrubs. According to an article in the September 13, 1979 edition of the *Morton Grove Champion* newspaper, the girls had intended to go shopping near the forest preserve and had taken Bender's car earlier in the day.

When Ovington did not show up for a 5:15pm date with her boyfriend, Joe Marjorus, he organized a search party. Marjorus was there when the bodies were discovered.

The Cook County Sheriff's police, Forest Preserve Rangers and Morton Grove Police stepped up patrols in the area and worked diligently on the case. At one point, the Morton Grove Police were using a hypnotist to question a witness that may have seen something on September 5th when the girls were killed. According to *The Morton Grove Champion* of October 18, 1979, they were looking for a blue car in relation to the murders. Bender's car was light blue and it was discovered at the Par-King miniature golf course parking lot. This was a different blue car that they were looking for. Several psychics had offered their help with the case and supplied such information as, "The girls had seen something they shouldn't have and that is why they were killed." The fact that valuables were left on the bodies of the girls tended to rule out robbery as a motive and an autopsy conducted ruled out sexual assault. A Sgt. McKenna with Morton Grove said that there was one psychic who was pretty well on the money as far as the murders were actually committed but stated that he couldn't get into specific details. McKenna did say that none of the information from the psychics had led to a break in the case yet.

Later, the Assistant State's Attorney assigned to the case, Dennis Wolter, confirmed to the *Chicago Tribune* in an article dated November 11, 1979, that a certain psychic in the case had provided useful information. He could not elaborate on the specifics of the information or the name of the psychic involved. According to the article, the psychic gave a description of the killer and told police that he would pass a lie detector test.

Based on the hypnosis of a single witness and the information provided by the unnamed psychic, the police zeroed in on a 19-year-old suspect named Matt Echols. Echols had been a Skokie resident until shortly after the murders when he moved to Arizona. His vehicle matched the description of the vehicle given by the witness including the missing chrome and mostly missing fender. The witness described Echols and another young man who ran out of the St. Paul Woods into the back parking lot of the Par-King miniature golf course where the slain girls' vehicle was also parked. Echols had also worked at a gas station in Skokie that was frequented by Bender and was a short distance from her home. The *Tribune* reported that a source close to the case had said that the psychic had given "a pretty good run-down on the killer."

Investigators from Morton Grove flew to Arizona to meet with Echols who was "uncooperative" during the interview and refused to take a lie detector test. The only thing the investigators had to go on was the description of the vehicle which matched, but they said that they couldn't place Echols' vehicle at the scene. I had attempted to contact the Morton Grove Police Department in an effort to obtain the psychic's name or confirm the claims of the newspaper articles but was denied a Freedom of Information Request due to the fact that the case was still under investigation. This case also remains unsolved.

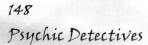

Case Notes:
Can Psychic Information Solve Crimes?

I have to side with psychic, Mel Doerr on this one. I can't say that psychics can or have ever solved crimes. In my experience, a combination of good police work, sloppy criminals, and a dose of old-fashioned good luck has solved the majority of crimes.

Keep in mind that I am not saying that psychics are frauds although they are out there. I have seen and experienced enough myself to lead me to believe that there is something to the concept of ESP or of clairvoyance or even precognition, but I don't think anyone has had the ability to prove it beyond a doubt or been able to control it to the point that it can be used reliably and specifically enough to be of use to investigators on a regular basis. Most reputable "sensitives" will tell you that they are not always right on with their impressions. I would assume that if someone had that much specific control over their gift that it would have been difficult to avoid the publicity that would almost certainly have followed. That is unless you are a hard core conspiracy theorist who believes that the CIA or some other more secretive government agency has an undisclosed think-tank of proven telepathics working in the interest of national security. That, however, is a different book for a different time!

Wrapping It Up

I told you in the introduction that I would meet you on the other side of the book and here we are. Hopefully you enjoyed reading the book as much as I enjoyed writing it.

There are just so many great examples of legends, folklore, and tales of the supernatural that come out of this great melting pot of over 200 distinct neighborhoods that we call, The City of Chicago. It is impossible to do them all justice in just one book. I guess that's why books have multiple editions and why I tried not to bite off more than I could chew.

Not only do numerous legends abound from years gone by but there are constantly new stories popping up daily that hope to become legend some day.

I didn't start out with the idea that I was going to "solve" anything in particular but I did want to delve a little deeper into some of the more well-known legends as well as some not so well-known and I think we have accomplished that.

Until the next case,
Ray Johnson

Bibliography and Suggested Readings

Archer, Fred. *Crime and the Psychic World*. New York, NY: W.Morrow, 1969.

Bielski, Ursula. *Chicago Haunts: Ghostlore of the Windy City*. Chicago,IL: Lake Claremont Press, 1998.

Blum, Deborah. *Ghost Hunters: William James and the Search for Scientific Proof of Life After Death*. New York, NY: Penguin Press, 2006.

Crowe, Richard T., and Carol Mercado. *Chicago's Street Guide to the Supernatural: A Guide to Haunted and Legendary Places In and Near the Windy City*. Oak Park, IL: Carolando Press, 2000.

Mercado, Carol. *A Voice From the Grave*. New York, NY: Diamond Books, 1994.

O'Brien, John, and Edward Baumann. Teresita. *The Voice From the Grave: The Incredible But True Story of How an Occult Vision Solved the Murder of Teresita Basa*. Chicago, IL: Bonus Books, 1992.

Posner, Gary P. "A Not-So-Psychic Detective." Skeptic (Vol.5 No.4, 1997):52.

Reiser, Martin; Ludwig, Louise; Saxe, Susan; and Wagner, Clare. "An Evaluation of the Use of Psychics in the Investigation of Major Crimes." *Journal of Police Science and Administration* (Vol.7 No.1, 1979):18.

Index

Index